9.50

OXFORD MEDIEVAL TEXTS

General Editors

V. H. GALBRAITH   R. A. B. MYNORS
C. N. L. BROOKE

LIBELLUS DE
DIVERSIS ORDINIBUS

de heremitis q̄ sepe sola uit cū p... ...
e diuisis ordinib; ut pfessionib; sermone
habituri que a religiosis uiris scōi ppłi
fugentib; in eccłia dō tēnenda uouent.
Pmō oportet ostendere qd̄ etiā pmaeual
dei seruitiū & cultū libens frequentauit.
Ibi enī abel sacrificiū acceptabile optulit. seth nōn̄
di cū sua pgenie inuocauit. noe q̄q; in sua genera
tiōe iustus inuent̄ & ad obediendū dō pnipt̄ ipso
iubente archā fabricauit. Vnde qꝛ ad heremitas
pncipiū sermonis facere disposuim. intueam̄ si for
te in pmis hominib; aliqm hoꝛ seruoꝛ dī similitu
dine inuenire potuerim. Na illos poꝛes homines
aliqñdo solos habuisse. eo indicio pdocem̄ qd̄ cain
occiso frē suo abel pmū legit ciuitatē edificasse. &
ex nomine filii sui enos eande appellasse. Testat̄ eñi
iosephus hoc ideo eū fecisse; qd̄ latrocinia exerce
ret. & ad eade scēm agenda familiares suos domes
ticosq; inū muros conuenire cogeret. Vnde constat
pmā illā etatē licet paruo tēpore multū innocent
uixisse. q̄b; nec edificandaꝝ domoꝛ adhuc cura erat
nec cibi potū... nc̄ e diligentia. nec uestiū uani
tas. nec auriū argentiq; tanta acqrendi sollertia;
Gramīnib; eñi & aq̄ simplici & arboꝛ fructib; uti dc̄s
dixerat utebant. Vña qꝺā facundissimi nī phylo
sophi laude pmoꝛ hominū carmine mirifico decantan
aut. Felix nimiū poꝛ etas contenta fidelib; aruis.

LIBELLUS DE DIVERSIS ORDINIBUS ET PROFESSIONIBUS QUI SUNT IN AECCLESIA

EDITED AND TRANSLATED
WITH INTRODUCTION AND NOTES
BY

G. CONSTABLE

AND

B. SMITH

OXFORD
AT THE CLARENDON PRESS
1972

Oxford University Press, Ely House, London W.1

GLASGOW   NEW YORK   TORONTO   MELBOURNE   WELLINGTON
CAPE TOWN   IBADAN   NAIROBI   DAR ES SALAAM   LUSAKA   ADDIS ABABA
DELHI   BOMBAY   CALCUTTA   MADRAS   KARACHI   LAHORE   DACCA
KUALA LUMPUR   SINGAPORE   HONG KONG   TOKYO

PRINTED IN GREAT BRITAIN
AT THE UNIVERSITY PRESS, OXFORD
BY VIVIAN RIDLER
PRINTER TO THE UNIVERSITY

PREFACE

THE two editors have co-operated closely in the preparation of this volume, but the introduction and the edition of the Latin text are primarily the work of Mr. Constable, and the translation of Mr. Smith. They are deeply indebted to Mr. Paul Meyvaert, of Duke University, now Executive Secretary of the Mediaeval Academy of America, for reviewing both the Latin text and the translation and above all for his invaluable assistance in the identification of references, and to Professor C. N. L. Brooke, who went over the entire volume with a critical and discerning eye. For further aid in identifying references and place-names, they are grateful to Dom Jean Becquet and Dom Paul Antin, both of Ligugé, to Dr. Ludo Milis of Ghent, and to Professor Roger Reynolds of Carleton University, Ottawa.

CONTENTS

ABBREVIATIONS

CC   *Corpus Christianorum* (Turnhout, 1954–)

CSEL   *Corpus scriptorum ecclesiasticorum latinorum* (Vienna and Prague, 1866–)

PL   *Patrologia latina*, ed. J. P. Migne (Paris, 1844–64)

INTRODUCTION

(i) *Background*

THE period from the middle of the eleventh century to the end of the twelfth marked a turning-point in the history of Christianity, and especially in the history of monasticism and other forms of organized religious life. The exact number of men and women living under a rule as monks, canons, hermits, and recluses is not known, but during this period it increased enormously in terms not only of absolute numbers, perhaps as much as ten-fold in some regions, but probably also of proportion to the total population, although this was a time of rapid demographic growth. Bishop Otto of Bamberg, who died in 1139, was said by his biographer Herbord to have given the increase in population as his reason for founding twenty houses of monks and canons in his own and other dioceses. 'At the beginning of the world,' in Otto is reported to have said, 'when there were few men, the propagation of men was necessary, and therefore they were not chaste, but everyone married and gave in marriage. Now, however, he said, at the end of the world, when men have multiplied beyond measure, is the time of chastity; whoever can must be chaste and devoted to God. But chastity and other works of sanctity can be better observed within monasteries than outside. This was my reason, he said, my intention in multiplying monasteries.'[1]

The effectiveness of monasticism as a means of demographic control, except among the upper classes, may be doubted, since the total percentage of the population living in monasteries can at no time have been very great; and there were obviously spiritual reasons, as Otto recognized, for the growth and diversity of religious orders and professions at that time. Many new types of

---

[1] Herbord of Michelsberg, *Dialogus de Ottone episcopo Bambergensi*, i. 18, in Ph. Jaffé, ed., *Bibliotheca rerum germanicarum*, v (Weimar, 1869), 717. Herbord's own monastery of Michelsberg at Bamberg grew from less than twenty at the beginning of Otto's episcopate to over seventy by 1121/3 and to about a hundred at the time Herbord was writing, in 1158: cf. Ebbo, *Vita Ottonis*, i. 20 (21), and Herbord, *Dialogus*, i, preface, in op. cit., pp. 610 and 706–7.

religious life were inspired by a desire to break away from the established values and institutional forms of monasticism and to withdraw from the world of feudal obligations and manorial organization into a more individualistic way of life dedicated to personal salvation and the spiritual and temporal service of others, whose needs were increasingly apparent in an age of growing social awareness and economic development. Otto of Bamberg devoted much of his energy and resources to caritative work, and on this account was forbidden to become a monk by Abbot Wulfram of Michelsberg. 'Who among monks is so perfect,' Wulfram asked, 'that his merit and poverty can be compared to your wealth?' After this, according to Otto's biographer, 'the diocese of Bamberg was turned entirely to alms, entirely to the care of the poor and pilgrims. Any grain or food, any gold or silver discovered anywhere at any time was transformed into heavenly treasures through the hands of the needy.'[1]

These efforts to find new forms of religious life, in and yet not of the world, culminated in the foundation of the mendicant orders in the thirteenth century; but many earlier groups and individuals, including not only monks but also canons, hermits, and members of military orders, and increasingly including women as well as men, were inspired by similar ideals, which seemed to embody the highest type of religious vocation.[2] Many members of older orders and monasteries naturally resented this challenge to the traditional concept of claustration and liturgical regularity, which necessarily involved a certain degree of dependance on the established social and economic order. There was a lively exchange of writings both attacking and defending the different types of religious life. Beginning with the *Libelli de lite*, which were concerned with the reform of the papacy, there emerged a new type of controversial literature designed to win the support of influential segments of society, although it would be premature to speak of anything like public opinion or propaganda in the modern senses of these terms.

As a genre, these writings have been comparatively little studied, and many of those concerned with the various forms of religious

[1] Herbord, *Dialogus*, i. 30, in *Bibliotheca rerum germanicarum*, v. 727.

[2] The best discussion of these religious movements, though old and concerned principally with the later Middle Ages, is Herbert Grundmann, *Religiöse Bewegungen im Mittelalter* (Berlin, 1935, reprinted, with additional material, Hildesheim, 1961).

life have only recently appeared in print or not yet been published at all. They are frequently cast in the form of a dialogue, treatise, letter, or commentary and often make use of traditional types of argument which tend to conceal their real purpose and meaning. The authors were usually angry as well as confused, and did not understand the causes of the differences between the forms of religious life which they were attacking or defending. Owing to their regard for custom and tradition, they spent their time in vituperative arguments over external observances, to which they attached an exaggerated moral importance. Basically, however, they were concerned with the question of the nature of the highest type of Christian life on earth, and buried in their works is a serious moral discussion, out of which emerged a reassessment which deeply influenced the later history of Christian spirituality.

(ii) *The Manuscript*

The *Libellus de diuersis ordinibus et professionibus qui sunt in aecclesia* is one of the most perceptive, impartial, and clearly organized examples of this type of religious controversial literature. Like many others, it survives in only one known manuscript, perhaps the writer's autograph, which was purchased by the British Museum in 1856 from C. Hamilton and is now numbered Add. 21244. It is a small volume consisting of thirty-five leaves of vellum measuring about 195 by 120 millimetres and pricked and ruled for either twenty-seven or twenty-eight lines per page. The leaves are gathered into four signatures of eight, ten, ten, and eight (which lacks the final leaf) leaves respectively and numbered with three sets of numbers: a foliation from cxxxv to clxviiii, in a thirteenth-century (?) hand, showing that the manuscript once formed part of a large volume; a late medieval pagination from 1 to 70; and a modern pencil foliation from 1 to 35. The signatures are bound in the wrong order, with the third before the second, and the medieval foliation shows that this error goes back to an early date. It was realized, but not corrected by rebinding, at the time of the second numbering, which may have coincided with the separation of the text from the works with which it was previously bound and which runs from 1 to 16 (the first signature), 37 to 56 (originally the third signature), 17 to 36 (originally the second signature), and 57 to 70 (the fourth signature). Probably

at the same time and by the same hand, notes and distinctive signs were placed in the text warning the reader to go from the present f. 8ᵛ forward to f. 19ʳ, back from f. 28ᵛ to 9ʳ, and then from f. 18ᵛ to f. 29ʳ. The signatures remained in the wrong order, however, when the manuscript was rebound in the nineteenth century, presumably at the time it entered the British Museum, and the modern foliation still perpetuates the medieval binding error.

The text is written in a clear and reasonably even twelfth-century hand and is decorated with a few capital letters in silver, red, and blue, and with occasional rubrications in the text. It was evidently written by the same scribe, but probably over a considerable period of time, to judge from the variations in the size of the script and the colour of the ink, in the number of lines per page, and in the pattern of the textual rubrications, which are found for all capital letters only on ff. 19ʳ–23ʳ (originally leaves 1–5 of the second signature). The presence in the text of some fifty small corrections and changes, written apparently in the same hand, suggests that the manuscript may be the author's autograph copy. This is also indicated by the fact that the manuscript contains only the first book of the *Libellus*. That the author planned to write at least one other book is clear from both the prologue and the conclusion, but it is missing here. This manuscript is either, therefore, a draft of the first book of a work of which the other book or books are lost or, more probably, the original and only copy of a work which is complete in itself but was never continued.[1]

The manuscript belonged in the late Middle Ages to the Benedictine abbey of St. James at Liège, as the colophon written on f. 35ᵛ in the fourteenth or fifteenth century shows: 'Explicit liber de diversis professionibus et ordinibus qui sunt in ecclesia. Qui pertinet monasterio sancti jacobi leodiensis ordinis sancti benedicti nigrorum monachorum.'[2] This provenance establishes almost beyond question that this was 'the ancient codex of St. James at Liège' used by Martène and Durand for the first printed edition of the text, which appeared in 1733 and was reprinted by Migne in the

---

[1] The appearance of the manuscript argues against the alternative that it is a scribal copy of the first book only from another manuscript.

[2] There is also an illegible 'gratinated' inscription at the top of f. 35ᵛ and a late-medieval title and press-mark of R·13 on f. 1ʳ.

Patrologia latina.[1] The manuscript was still at Liège in the early eighteenth century, therefore, but exactly when and how it came to England is not known.

(iii) *The Author*

The only internal indications of authorship are in the salutation and prologue, which show that the author's name began with R and that he was a canon, since he gave this as his reason for not discussing the canons first in his treatise.[2] The type of canon is less certain. He was clearly not a secular canon of the type described in pejorative tones in Part VII. His moderate and tolerant tone, especially with regard to fasting and diversity of customs, also suggests that he was not a strict regular canon of the type described, with obvious admiration, in Part V. It therefore seems probable that he was one of the regular canons described in Part VI as living near to, but not among, laymen. The correspondent to whom the *Libellus* was addressed, however, and whose name also began with R, was clearly a monk, since the author specifically refers to his having become a monk and living under the rule of an abbot.[3]

The work can be dated, apart from the script of the manuscript, from the reference in the title of Part V to the canons of Prémontré, which was founded in 1121, and of Saint-Josse-au-Bois, which moved to Dommartin in 1161.[4]

Putting together this internal evidence with the provenance of the manuscript, scholars have concluded that the author of the *Libellus* was a regular canon active at Liège, preferably connected with St. James, about the middle of the twelfth century. The most promising candidate (who seems to have been first proposed as the possible writer of the *Libellus* by Dereine in 1947)[5] is Reimbald (Raimbald, Rimbald), who was a canon of St. John the Evangelist at Liège early in the twelfth century, a canon of St. Lambert in

---

[1] Edmond Martène and Ursin Durand, *Veterum scriptorum . . . amplissima collectio* (Paris, 1724–33), ix. 1027–74, reprinted in *PL*, ccxiii. 807–50.

[2] p. 2 (Prologue).   [3] pp. 24–6 (chap. 13).   [4] See below, p. 57 n. 1.

[5] Charles Dereine, 'Les origines de Prémontré', *Revue d'histoire ecclésiastique*, xlii (1947), 359–60; cf. idem, 'Enquête sur la règle de saint Augustin', *Scriptorium*, ii (1947–8), 34; 'Les coutumiers de Saint-Quentin de Beauvais et de Springiersbach', *Revue d'histoire ecclésiastique*, xliii (1948), 442 n. 1; and 'L'école canonique liégeoise et la réforme grégorienne', *Miscellanea Tornacensia*, ed. J. Cassart (Brussels, 1951) i. 92. Dereine dates the work to 1125/30.

1116, provost of St. John the Evangelist from 1126 to 1140, provost of the Holy Cross and dean of St. Lambert from 1141 until his death in 1149.[1] He appears frequently in documents and other sources for the history of Liège in the first half of the twelfth century, and he wrote several works of spirituality and history which have recently been re-edited by De Clercq. Although he had no known personal connections with the abbey of St. James, his father Ralph of Dongelberg granted some lands at Roloux to St. James in 1101.[2] Dereine's suggestion that he wrote the *Libellus* has much to recommend it, therefore, and found immediate favour with scholars. Among those who have followed it, with varying degrees of confidence, are Dickinson, De Warren (calling Reimbald a Premonstratensian), Chenu, Laporte, Leclercq, Meersseman, and Severino.[3] Delhaye, writing in 1947, proposed that the *Libellus* was 'very probably' written by a Premonstratensian; Frugoni in 1961 suggested the somewhat unlikely name of Anselm of Havelberg; and both Genicot and Fonseca referred to the treatise as anonymous.[4] De Clercq in his edition of the works

---

[1] Jacques Stiennon, *Étude sur le chartrier et le domaine de l'abbaye de Saint-Jacques de Liège (1015–1209)* (Bibliothèque de la Faculté de Philosophie et Lettres de l'Université de Liège, 124; Paris, 1951), p. 300, and Reimbald of Liège, *Opera omnia*, ed. C. de Clercq (*CC*: Continuatio mediaeualis, 4; Turnholt, 1966), p. v.

[2] Stiennon, *Saint-Jacques*, pp. 299–304.

[3] J. C. Dickinson, *The Origins of the Austin Canons and their Introduction into England* (London, 1950), p. 63; H.-B. de Warren, in *Bernard de Clairvaux* (Commission d'histoire de l'ordre de Cîteaux, 3; Paris, 1953), p. 62; M.-D. Chenu, *La Théologie au douzième siècle* (Études de philosophie médiévale, 45; Paris, 1957), p. 227; [M. Laporte], *Aux sources de la vie cartusienne* (La Chartreuse, 1960 ff.) ii. 201; Jean Leclercq, *Études sur le vocabulaire monastique du Moyen Age* (Studia Anselmiana, 48; Rome, 1961), pp. 19 n. 48, and 98 n. 81; G. G. Meersseman, 'Eremitismo e predicazione itinerante dei secoli XI e XII', *L'eremitismo in Occidente nei secoli XI e XII* (Pubblicazioni dell'Università Cattolica del Sacro Cuore, Contributi, 3 s.: Miscellanea del Centro di Studi Medioevali, 4; Milan, 1965), pp. 166–7; idem, 'I penitenti nei secoli XI e XII', *I laici nella 'Societas christiana' dei secoli XI e XII* (Pubblicazioni dell'Università Cattolica del Sacro Cuore, Contributi, 3 s.: Miscellanea del Centro di Studi Medioevali, 5; Milan, 1968), p. 337; Gabriella Severino, 'La discussione degli "Ordines" di Anselmo di Havelberg', *Bullettino dell'Istituto Storico Italiano per il Medio Evo*, lxxviii (1967), 105–6.

[4] Philippe Delhaye, 'L'Organisation scolaire au XIIe siècle', *Traditio*, v (1947), 213 n. 12; Arsenio Frugoni, 'Momenti del problema dell'*ordo laicorum* nei secoli X–XII', *Nova historia*, xiii (1961), 21; Léopold Genicot, 'L'érémitisme du XIe siècle dans son contexte économique et social', *L'eremitismo*, p. 47 n. 5; and C. D. Fonseca, 'Discorso di apertura', *I laici*, p. 15 (calling it 'di ambiente premonstratense') and 'I conversi nelle comunità canonicali', ibid., p. 263 n. 4.

of Reimbald of Liège made no reference to the *Libellus*. Scholarly opinion on the matter is far from unanimous, therefore, but it seems fair to say that the predominant view is that the *Libellus* was probably written by Reimbald.

Against this opinion is the important fact that the text seems to show very little resemblance in content or style to the known works of Reimbald. In particular, Reimbald's learned style and occasionally sharp tone and partisan views are in contrast with the moderate and practical position of the author of the *Libellus*, whose personal sympathies are sometimes hard to determine from the descriptions he gives of the various religious orders. Reimbald uses the terms 'ordo' and 'professio' more loosely than they are used in the *Libellus*. He makes no reference to hermits in his known works, only one to monks, and derives 'the order of clerics' from the apostles. He lays greater emphasis than the author of the *Libellus* on episcopal control and distinguishes 'the two types of clerics' as those 'living under episcopal rule' and those without a head.[1] The types of sources used by Reimbald and in the *Libellus* also differ. Reimbald, for instance, cites extensively from canonical sources, which are not used at all in the *Libellus*, but he makes no references to the Benedictine Rule and relatively fewer than the *Libellus* to Jerome and certain specific books of the Bible.[2] Although these points are individually inconclusive, together they throw considerable doubt on the attribution of the *Libellus* to Reimbald.

There were many other canons with names beginning with R active at Liège in the first half of the twelfth century, though Reimbald is the only known writer among them. There were canons named Richard at St. Peter, St. Martin, and the Holy Cross, Ralph at St. Peter and the Holy Cross, Renzo at St. Lambert and St. Peter, Robert at the Holy Cross, Rudolf at St. Peter, Reinerus at St. Lambert, and many others.[3] An attractive candidate for

---

[1] Reimbald, *Opera*, p. 56 and in index, s.v. *ordo* (p. 174) and *professio* (p. 176).

[2] Ibid., index auctorum (pp. 143–55).

[3] Cf. Edgar de Marneffe, 'Tableau chronologique des dignitaires du chapitre Saint-Lambert à Liège [i]', *Analectes pour servir à l'histoire ecclésiastique de la Belgique*, xxv (1895), 446–8 (Renzo) and *passim*; Édouard Poncelet, *Inventaire analytique des chartes de la collégiale de Saint-Pierre à Liège* (Académie royale de Belgique: Commission royale d'histoire; Brussels, 1905), pp. lxxxii (Richard, Rudolf) and 5 (Ralph, Renzo); idem, *Inventaire analytique des chartes de la collégiale de Sainte-Croix à Liège* (Académie royale de Belgique: Commission

the recipient of the *Libellus*, or even the author, is a certain Richer who at the turn of the twelfth century was a canon at St. Denis and later became a monk of St. James, where he died in 1126.[1] Reimbald himself dedicated his *De vita canonica* to the 'abbas canonicus' Richer of Rolduc.[2] Also at Rolduc, in 1130, was a recluse named Reinwidis.[3] Any of these R's might have written the *Libellus*. Unless further evidence comes to light, however, not even the localization to Liège can be considered certain, since the manuscript may have been taken there after it was written, and the identity of the author will remain unknown.

(iv) *The Historical Context*

Apart from these specific clues to the authorship of the *Libellus*, however, there are various indications in the text that it originated in north-eastern France or the Low Countries in the twelfth century. The diocese of Liège was a recognized centre of religious and intellectual activity at that time,[4] and together with its neighbouring dioceses in the province of Rheims showed a degree of ferment in the life of its religious institutions hardly equalled anywhere else in Europe. A glance through the documents collected by Miraeus gives an idea of the number of old religious houses which were reformed and of new ones established in the late eleventh and twelfth centuries.[5] The tensions between the old and new types of canons, which have been studied by Dereine in the period before St. Norbert,[6] were heightened by the coming of the Premonstratensians, who enjoyed a great success in both the dioceses of Liège and Cambrai in the 1120s and were

royale d'histoire; Brussels, 1911) i. 12 (Ralph, Richard, Robert, Renzo), 11 (Richard), 18 (Robert); etc. In addition to the cathedral, there were seven collegiate churches at Liège.

[1] J. F. Niermeyer, *Onderzoekingen over Luikse en Maastrichtse oorkonden en over de Vita Baldrici episcopi Leodiensis* (Diss. Utrecht; Groningen, 1935), p. 86; Stiennon, *Saint-Jacques*, p. 269.

[2] Reimbald, *Opera*, p. 9; Stiennon, *Saint-Jacques*, p. 300.

[3] E. van Wintershoven, 'Recluseries et ermitages dans l'ancien diocèse de Liège', *Bulletin de la Société scientifique et littéraire du Limbourg*, xxiii (1905), 114.

[4] Cf. Reimbald, *Chronicon rythmicum Leodiense*, ll. 214–15, in *Opera*, p. 130: 'Religio uiget Leodij / discipline, artes, fons studij.'

[5] A. Miraeus [Le Mire], *Opera diplomatica*, ed. J. F. Foppens (Brussels, 1723–48).

[6] Charles Dereine, *Les Chanoines réguliers au diocèse de Liège avant saint Norbert* (Académie royale de Belgique: Classe des lettres, Mémoires in-8°, 2 s., 47. 1; Brussels, 1952), pp. 23–7.

particularly patronized by Bishop Albero I of Liège (1123–8).[1] The Cistercians established their first houses in this region a few years later, and between 1132 and 1148 five abbeys were founded or taken over by the Cistercians, four of them owing to the personal intervention of St. Bernard.[2]

The older orders of monks and canons continued to hold their own in spite of the advances of the reformers, however. Rupert of Deutz, for example, who spent much of his life at Liège, was a vigorous proponent of the principles of old black Benedictine monasticism.[3] The introduction and spread of Cluniac priories in the diocese of Liège in the late eleventh and early twelfth centuries also shows the vitality of the old forms of monasticism, and the support given to them by the nobles of the region.[4] The old houses of canons likewise continued to flourish, and there was no serious decline in the standard of canonical life before the beginning of the thirteenth century.[5] In the period before the coming of the Premonstratensians, the foundation of such houses as Flône, Saint-Gilles, Neufmoustier, and Rolduc is a sign in this area of the apparently spontaneous movement of eremitical and hospitaler life, of which the effects were felt all over northern Europe and which continued at least until the middle of the twelfth century.[6]

This situation seems to correspond to the variety of forms of religious life described in the *Libellus*. The correspondence might be even closer if we had the second book which the author mentions in the prologue and in which he planned to discuss, first, the male recluses and so-called *licoisi* who lived a religious

[1] A. Cauchie, 'Lettre de Frédéric, archevêque de Cologne, à Albéron Ier, évêque de Liège, concernant l'établissement des Prémontrés (1125)', *Analectes pour servir à l'histoire ecclésiastique de la Belgique*, xxxv (1909), 285–8.

[2] Joseph-Marie Canivez, *L'Ordre de Cîteaux en Belgique des origines (1132) au XXme siècle* (Forges lez-Chimay, 1926), pp. 65–113.

[3] On Rupert, see the recent article, with extensive references, by Hubert Silvestre, 'Notes sur la controverse de Rupert de Saint-Laurent avec Anselme de Laon et Guillaume de Champeaux', *Saint-Laurent de Liège*, ed. Rita Lejeune (Liège [1968]), pp. 63–80.

[4] Joseph Halkin, 'Les prieurés clunisiens de l'ancien diocèse de Liège', *Bulletin de la Société d'art et d'histoire du diocèse de Liège*, x (1896), 155–293, and E. de Moreau, *Histoire de l'église en Belgique*, ii, 2nd edn. (Museum Lessianum: Section historique, 2; Brussels, n.d.), p. 179.

[5] Dereine, *Chanoines*, pp. 48–52, and Édouard Poncelet, 'La cessation de la vie commune dans les églises canoniales de Liège', *Annuaire d'histoire liégeoise*, iv. 5 (1952), 613–48.

[6] Dereine, *Chanoines*, pp. 105–245, esp. 237–8.

life without being formally either hermits, monks, canons, or recluses and, second, the female hermits, nuns, recluses, and *licoisae*. Much less is known about these less organized types of religious life than about the monks and canons; but it is known that women played an exceptionally important part in religious life and thought in the diocese of Liège in the twelfth century, both as nuns, canonesses, hermits, and recluses.[1] The widow of Thiebald of Fouron, named Guda, for instance, who was a generous benefactor of the abbey of St. James, lived there for several years as a recluse before her death in 1125.[2]

The remarks in the *Libellus* concerning the desirability of uniformity in monastic and canonical usages, at least within each ecclesiastical province, in order to avoid dispute and scandal,[3] may be compared with a charter of Bishop Albero II of Liège in 1144 for the ancient monastery of Aulne, which had become a house of canons at the time of the Norman invasions and which the Abbot Ralph now wished to change (in the words of the charter) 'from the common life of clerics to the plan of a regular life'. The bishop gave his consent on condition, among other things, that the habit of the new regular canons 'should be such as to give no occasion for vanity and to savour in no way of novelty or superfluity'. In particular he stipulated that their hoods and surplices should not convey any criticism or blame of other canons, 'so that if by chance they should enter our convent [i.e. the cathedral chapter of St. Lambert], they should not differ from us owing to the novelty of their habit'.[4] This unusual desire to promote uniformity and prevent invidious comparisons, while still promoting reform, seems to parallel the concerns of the author of the *Libellus*.

Three specific features of the *Libellus* point more positively to its having originated in north-eastern France or the Low Countries.

---

[1] Van Wintershoven, in *Bull. Soc. scient. et litt. du Limbourg*, xxiii. 97–158, who comments that most of the recluses were women and most of the hermits, men; Dereine, *Chanoines*, pp. 239–40.

[2] H. Demaret, 'Guda, veuve de Thiebauld comte de Fouron, recluse à Saint-Jacques au commencement du XII⁰ siècle', *Bulletin de la Société d'art et d'histoire du diocèse de Liège*, iv (1886), 36–50; Stiennon, *Saint-Jacques*, pp. 322–3 and s.v. in index.

[3] p. 36 (chap. 19).

[4] Miraeus–Foppens, *Opera*, ii. 823–4; cf. Dereine, *Chanoines*, pp. 231–2, citing a more recent edition of this charter. This effort at reform was apparently a failure, since three years later Bishop Henry of Liège entrusted Aulne to St. Bernard and it became the second Cistercian abbey (after Villers in 1146) in the diocese of Liège: Canivez, *L' Ordre de Cîteaux*, pp. 94 ff.

First, the list of orders through which Christ is said to have progressed (the so-called Ordinal of Christ) is distinctive in three
ways: (1) the usual order of the grades of *ostiarius* and *lector* are
reversed, (2) the grade of bishop, which appears in most twelfth-
century lists of this sort, is omitted, and (3) the sanction for the
grade of subdeacon is given as Christ's ministration, which is
found in no other known Ordinal of Christ.[1] In general, the
sanctions of the individual grades resemble those given by the
Norman Anonymous more closely than those in other known
ordinals; and it seems that the author of the *Libellus*, the Norman
Anonymous, and several other writers of the school of Bec may
have used a lost form of the Ordinal current in the north of
France. This view is supported by the reference to the duty of the
subdeacon to minister in a fragment of the *De officiis septem gra-
duum* in the tenth-century *Pontificale Lanaletense* now at Rouen.[2]

Second, the textual variants in the passages from Augustine's
letter 54 cited in the *Libellus* are closer to those from St. Omer
311 (of the eleventh or twelfth century) than from any other
manuscript listed in the apparatus to Goldbacher's edition of the
letters of St. Augustine.[3] The passages from Boethius also include
some distinctive variants, which might help to localize the textual
tradition used by the author of the *Libellus*, but they do not appear
in the apparatus of any available edition of the *Consolatio*.

A third feature which may be cited besides these two textual
features suggesting a northern origin is the interesting passage
in the *Libellus* concerning monastic estates.[4] The *hospites* and
terrae hospitales which certain monks are said to grant *ad censum*
and in return for rents indicate a distinctive and relatively privi-
leged type of land tenure often associated with the opening of
new lands and found particularly in northern France and Lower
Lorraine.[5] The *Libellus* also refers to *seruos et ancillas capitales*

---

[1] The Ordinal appears twice in the *Libellus*, on pp. 10–12 (chap. 4) and, in
reverse order, on p. 60 (chap. 33). Professor Roger Reynolds of Carleton
University in Ottawa has kindly supplied the information given here on the
Ordinals of Christ.

[2] *Pontificale Lanaletense* (*Bibliothèque de la ville de Rouen, A.27. Cat. 368*).
A Pontifical formerly in use at St. Germans, Cornwall, ed. G. H. Doble (Henry
Bradshaw Society, 74; London, 1937), p. 41, l. 25.

[3] pp. 34–6 (chap. 18).   [4] pp. 40–2 (chap. 20).

[5] Cf. B.-E.-C. Guérard, *Cartulaire de l'abbaye de Saint-Père de Chartres*
(Collection de documents inédits sur l'histoire de France; Paris, 1840) i, pp.
xxxv–xxxvi; Achille Luchaire, *Histoire des institutions monarchiques de la France*

on ecclesiastical lands and describes how serfs and *hospites* flee from their cruel lords to the *dominium* of churches and monasteries, which receive them, according to the author, out of mercy rather than cupidity and so establish 'cities of fugitives in the possession of the saints'. The monks act in place of Caesar for these fugitives by protecting their persons, families, and possessions, and they are therefore justified in receiving from them the dues owing to Caesar.[1] The precise legal position of these dependants is not clear in the *Libellus*, but they obviously resemble the *sainteurs* (*censuales*, *tributarii*, *capitales*) over whose status there has been a lively debate among scholars. They were essentially men and women living under the protection of a saint, in the form of a church or monastery, and paying as a sign of this dependency a small annual *census capitis* and specific payments at death and marriage, in addition to recognizing the secular jurisdiction of the church.[2] These *tributarii*, according to Boeren, were 'the objects

sous les premiers Capétiens (987–1180), 2nd edn. (Paris, 1891) ii. 134–5; Henri Sée, *Les Classes rurales et le régime domanial en France au Moyen Âge* (Bibliothèque internationale d'économie politique; Paris, 1901), pp. 224–38; Léo Verriest, *Le Servage dans le comté de Hainaut. Les sainteurs. Le meilleur catel.* (Académie royale de Belgique: Classe des lettres, Mémoires in-8°, 2 s., 6; Brussels, 1910), pp. 28–31. A monk of Morigny in the early twelfth century gathered almost eighty 'hospites oblatiarios' to cultivate a long-neglected estate at Maisons-en-Beauce, near Chartres: *La Chronique de Morigny*, ed. Léon Mirot, 2nd edn. (Collection de textes pour servir à l'étude et à l'enseignement de l'histoire, 41; Paris, 1912), p. 6. Du Cange thought that these *hospites* of Morigny were monks, but they were probably 'colons volontaires', according to Ursmer Berlière, *La Familia dans les monastères bénédictins du Moyen Age* (Académie royale de Belgique: Classe des lettres, Mémoires in-8°, 2 s., 29. 2; Brussels, 1931), p. 81. Most of the examples of *hospites* given in these works, and in medieval Latin dictionaries, are from the north; and there are no references to *hospites* in the exhaustive works of C.-E. Perrin on the rural *seigneurie* in Upper Lorraine and of André Déléage on rural life in Burgundy.

[1] The idea that the fugitives themselves established the monks as civil authorities ('quos fugitiui ipsi Cesares . . . constituerunt') may be compared to the concept expounded by Manegold of Lautenbach that emperors and kings were created not by themselves but by the people over whom they ruled: cf. R. W. and A. J. Carlyle, *A History of Mediaeval Political Theory in the West* (Edinburgh–London, 1950) iii. 163–9, and the translations in Brian Tierney, *The Crisis of Church and State 1050–1300* (Englewood Cliffs, 1964), pp. 78–80.

[2] Verriest, *Servage*, pp. 171–248; Jean Paquay, 'La condition sociale des sainteurs dans la Limbourg aux xie, xiie et xiiie siècles', *Bulletin de la Société scientifique et littéraire du Limbourg*, xxviii (1910), 243–80; P. C. Boeren, *Étude sur les tributaires d'Église dans le comté de Flandre du IXe au XIVe siècle* (Uitgave van het Instituut voor Middeleeuwsche Geschiedenis der Keizer Karel Universiteit te Nijmegen, 3; Amsterdam, 1936); Stiennon, *Saint-Jacques*, pp. 305–7, with references to further literature on the dispute over whether the *sainteurs*

of the *dominium* of a church', rather than of a lay lord, and their status was 'a lasting guarantee against the danger of full lay serfdom'.[1]

(v) *The Author's Point of View and Method*

The most remarkable feature of the *Libellus*, however, is not its factual descriptions of the various ways of religious life but its analysis of the spiritual tendencies of these movements. The author's perception that the fundamental distinction was not between the orders of hermits, monks, and canons but between the strict, moderate, and lax groups within each order, and that the fundamental similarity, therefore, was between the similar tendencies in each order, gives the *Libellus* a special place among the twelfth-century treatises on religious life and is an insight still not fully appreciated by scholars who are primarily concerned with establishing the precise differences between the various orders.

The author's method of analysis is one which may not particularly appeal to modern readers but which was characteristic of the twelfth century. It consists in finding parallels in both the Old and the New Testaments for each of the callings within the religious orders of his day. He usually refers to these parallels as similarities (*similitudo, simile, assimilare*), but his occasional use of *exemplum* and *species* shows that he also thought in terms of a more formal relation between the Biblical prototypes and the contemporary activities. The exact texts which he chose to exemplify each of the callings are shown on the accompanying table. Some of them, especially the elaborate comparisons between the three types of canons and the three families of Levites described in the Book of Numbers, may appear fanciful and far-fetched today, and they certainly make difficult reading. 'The most rewarding approach to material of this sort', as Paul Meyvaert said of the use of Scripture by Gregory the Great, 'is to view it as a grand exercise in the use of the imagination, and not to

---

were basically servile or free. If the dependants referred to in the *Libellus* were *sainteurs*, it lends support to the view of Vanderkindere, Bloch, and Boeren, against that of Verriest, Paquay, Lamy, and Rolland, that they were fundamentally serfs.

[1] Boeren, *Tributaires*, pp. 22 and 44.

Table of Biblical Parallels

Part	Order or calling	Old Test. reference	Old Testament parallel	New Test. reference	New Testament parallel
I	Hermits	Genesis and Josephus	Abel in first age; patriarchs in second age	John 6: 15	Christ withdrew into mountain
II	Monks living close to laymen	1 Kgs. 10: 5–6	Prophets coming down from hill next to garrison of Philistines	John 11: 54	Christ withdrew with disciples to Ephrem near desert
III	Monks living far from laymen	3 Kgs. 18: 3–4	Prophets hidden in caves by Abdias	Luke 4: 42; Luke 6: 12	Christ went to pray in desert and mountain
IV	'Secular' monks	—	—	—	—
V	Canons living far from laymen	Num. 4: 15	Caathites serving inside sanctuary	John 19: 17–18	Christ carried cross to Calvary
VI	Canons living close to laymen:	Num. 4: 25–6	Gersonites:	Luke 22: 40–6	Christ prayed on Mount of Olives; agony in the garden; disciples followed Him
	(1) in cloister, occupied with internal things		(1) concerned with interior things only		
	(2) in cloister, but go out and care for guests and pilgrims		(2) concerned with interior and exterior things		
	(3) live outside cloister in dependencies and parishes		(3) concerned with exterior things		
VII	'Secular' canons, living among laymen	Num. 4: 31–2	Merarites caring for outer courtyard	Luke 22: 10–13	Christ ordered disciples to enter Jerusalem and to prepare for Pasch

worry overmuch about the actual text he is commenting on. Gregory was anxious to make certain doctrinal points, or to get across some of the lessons drawn from his own spiritual experience, and he was constantly on the watch for a Scriptural verse on which he could "peg" this or that idea. The more "pegs" he used—and they are often incongruous ones—to stress one particular point . . . the more we can be certain that this was a real preoccupation with him.'[1]

The Biblical texts used in the *Libellus* are thus an indication of the author's desire to justify the diversity of orders and callings in the Church as part of God's plan. The important point for him in chapter four of the Book of Numbers was that the Caathites, Gersonites, and Merarites, though leading different lives and performing different functions, were all members of the same family and were ordered by God to perform their respective duties. Neither their differences, therefore, nor those of their modern counterparts among the canons, could be considered in any way improper or illegitimate. The theme of diversity within unity went back at least to Gregory the Great in medieval thought and theology.[2] It was often cited in the polemics between the various religious orders in the twelfth century and, although not specifically mentioned by the author of the *Libellus*, it underlies much of his thought. He said of the hermits, for example: 'If it displeases you that all men of this calling do not live the same way, look at the creation fashioned by the good Creator in various ways and see how a harmony has been achieved from different chords.'[3]

More striking than his Old Testament parallels, however, are the examples drawn from the life of Christ, who represented the supreme unity in contrast to the apparent diversity of the various forms of religious life. For the author of the *Libellus*, the New Testament prototypes of the religious orders were not the apostles

[1] Paul Meyvaert, 'Gregory the Great and the Theme of Authority', *Spode House Review*, iii (no. 25) (1966), 5.

[2] Idem, 'Diversity within Unity, a Gregorian Theme', *Heythrop Journal*, iv (1963), 141–62; Hubert Silvestre, *'Diversi sed non adversi'*, *Recherches de théologie ancienne et médiévale*, xxxi (1964), 124–32, esp. p. 125 n. 4, on its use in twelfth-century religious polemics.

[3] p. 16 (chap. 7); cf. p. 28 (chap. 15), where he says with regard to differences in food, clothing, and manual labour: 'I desire to show that, although they live differently, they aspire from the one beginning to the one end which is Christ.'

or John the Baptist, as in early medieval spirituality, but the activities of Christ Himself when at different times in His life He withdrew from the world, entered Jerusalem for the Last Supper, and carried His cross up to Calvary. As in the Ordinals of Christ, where He fulfilled in His own person all the functions of the divine ministry, so likewise Christ justified the various forms of contemporary religious life.

This concentration on the person of Christ was characteristic of twelfth-century spirituality. The author of the *Libellus* refers repeatedly not only to the example of Christ's life but also, in warm and affectionate tones, to the humanity of 'my' and 'our' Christ and Jesus. His devotion to the body of Christ is of special interest because the feast of Corpus Christi originated a century later in the diocese of Liège.[1] He asserted in particular the clean and uncorrupted nature of Christ's body as consumed in the Eucharist. 'Such is the body of Christ I believe in, hold, embrace, consume, absorb into my innermost entrails', he declared. 'I love the veneration for His body', he said, and maintained that anyone who loved Christ's humility and adversity should take pleasure in his own 'worship and devotion for the body of Christ'.[2]

Further distinctive touches of twelfth-century spirituality appear throughout the *Libellus*. The need for a 'mixed' life of action and contemplation, for instance, was a theme close to the hearts of reformers in the twelfth century.[3] The interesting view that monks who lived close to laymen, like the Cluniacs, and were supported by alms and parochial revenues could therefore devote themselves purely to contemplation is echoed in the anonymous *Dialogue between a Cluniac and a Cistercian Monk*, where the Cluniacs, who performed no manual labour, were called contemplative and the Cistercians, who supported themselves, active.[4] The emphasis on the importance of good example is also characteristic.[5] 'He who lives well seems to me to evangelize better than

---

[1] Cf. F. Baix and C. Lambot, *La Dévotion à l'Eucharistie et le viiᵉ centenaire de la Fête-Dieu* (Gembloux–Namur [1946]) and F. Callaey, 'Origine e sviluppo della festa del "Corpus Domini"', *Euntes docete*, x (1957), 1–33, esp. 11.

[2] p. 70 (chap. 40).

[3] pp. 28–30 (chap. 15) and 40–2 (chap. 20).

[4] p. 18 (chap. 8); *Dialogus inter Cluniacensem monachum et Cisterciensem*, 5 in Edmond Martène and Ursin Durand, *Thesaurus novus anecdotorum* (Paris, 1717), v. 1574.

[5] Cf. Giovanni Miccoli, *Chiesa gregoriana* (Storici antichi e moderni, N.S. 17; Florence, 1966), pp. 85, 93, 109, and 255, and the unpublished Harvard Ph.D.

he who speaks well.'[1] And in speaking of hermits, the author said that 'the fruits of that life can be acquired without the name but the name alone is empty without the life'.[2] This point was much disputed at the time. Philip of Harvengt argued that a man's way of life has nothing to do with his name (what he is, in the sense of his formal profession). Rupert of Deutz, on the other hand, agreed on this point with the author of the *Libellus* and said that what a man does determines what he is.[3]

In spite of his tolerant and impartial tone and his determination to find what good he could in each religious order, the author of the *Libellus* was far from approving everything, and he was as ready to condemn those who clung blindly to 'the chalice of ingrained custom' and refused to change their old ways[4] as he was to condemn those members of the new orders who criticized without charity and created scandal by their innovations. Nor was he simply an apologist for the *status quo*. His high praise for the monks and canons who lived far from other men, and the Biblical prototypes he chose for them, can leave no doubt of his admiration and sympathy for the reformers, even though he doubted whether their standards and ideals should be applied to all other orders and callings in the Church.

(vi) *The Present Edition*

The Latin text of the *Libellus* is printed here from British Museum MS. Add. 21244, following as closely as possible the spelling and punctuation of the manuscript. The orthography is on the whole clear and consistent, with just enough variations to show that the writer had no abstract regard for uniformity. He usually writes ę, which has been expanded to *ae*, but at one point in the manuscript (ff. 13ᵛ–14ʳ) he spells *faederis* within twenty lines once with an *e* and three times with an ę. On f. 24ᵛ he spells *assequuntur* both with a *qu* and, on the next line, with a *c*; and within nine lines on

thesis (1969) of Caroline W. Bynum, '*Docere verbo et exemplo*: An Aspect of Twelfth Century Spirituality'.

[1] p. 94 (chap. 55).   [2] p. 14 (chap. 5).

[3] Philip of Harvengt, *De institutione clericorum*, iv (113), in *PL*, cciii. 817–18; Rupert of Deutz, *Altercatio monachi et clerici quod liceat monacho praedicare*, PL, clxx. 539–40. For a fuller discussion of this point, see Giles Constable, *Monastic Tithes from their Origins to the Twelfth Century* (Cambridge Studies in Medieval Life and Thought, N.S. 10; Cambridge, 1964), pp. 158–60 and 173–5.

[4] p. 88 (chap. 49).

f. 36ᵛ he spells *suppellectilem* twice with one *p* and once with a double *p*. *Jesus* is regularly spelled with an *h* for the *e*, and *nichil* spelled out with *ch*. *Michi* is once spelled out with *ch* (f. 8ᵛ) and abbreviations have been expanded accordingly. *Aequiperare* is spelled out on f. 12ʳ, and the abbreviation *p̄* has therefore been expanded as *per* even in words where *par* might have been indicated, but not in words, such as *corpalia*, where *por* is called for. Numerals have been spelled out when they are accompanied in the manuscript by abbreviation marks, like .xx̊.ii̊. Otherwise they have been left as numerals.

The punctuation of the manuscript has been preserved, except for a very few obvious errors or slips of the pen. Since the only major divisions in the text are the divisions into books, and some of the sentences are very long and elaborate, the reader would doubtless be aided by breaking down the text into paragraphs and shorter sentences and by supplementary punctuation. But this would almost certainly distort the intention of the writer, whose reference at one point to *auditores* shows that he expected the work to be read aloud and heard rather than read silently.[1] The purpose of the punctuation was to emphasize the pauses, rhythm, and emphasis of the speaker, therefore, rather than to assist the visual comprehension of the silent reader.[2]

The textual apparatus consists almost entirely of corrections, emendations, and additions made by the writer (who was, as explained above, very likely also the author). A few of these may be simply scribal errors which do not deserve to be recorded, but they are mostly amplifications, alternatives, and clarifications of the text. They have therefore all been incorporated into the printed text, and the variants indicate the original readings. These changes were not recorded by Martène in his edition.

A comparison of Martène's text with the manuscript also showed up some 200 textual errors, of which about seventy-five involved the omission or addition of whole words or phrases, including five *non*s. These seem to have been the result of hasty reading and copying, and the added words were mostly in order to make sense of passages which would otherwise have been incomprehensible. Having omitted the word *ordinem* before *uniuscuiusque monasterii*

---

[1] p. 100 (chap. 59).
[2] Cf. the remarks of R. W. Southern in his edition of Eadmer, *The Life of St Anselm* (Medieval Texts; London, 1962), pp xxviii–xxxiv.

on p. 28 (chap. 14), for example, Martène added *legem* after *monasterii*. On p. 48 (chap. 24), apparently owing to having misread *uir* for *uitae*, he changed the phrase 'caritas principis eis necessaria uitae subministrabat' to 'caritate principis eis necessaria uir fortissimus subministrabat'. And on p. 64 (chap. 35), having misread the final *ē* on *preciosiorem* as *est*, he inserted a *quae* before the *omni*. Apart from the omissions of negations and a few others, these errors do not seriously affect the meaning of the text as it was published by Martène and Migne, but they are a justification for this new edition.

Martène also divided the text into numbered paragraphs or chapters which are not found in the manuscript. Some of these clearly do not correspond to breaks which were intended by the author, and one (chap. 50) is inserted into the middle of a sentence. These chapters are well established in references to the *Libellus*, however, and are convenient for the reader, and they have therefore been preserved in the margins of the present edition and in cross references to the text.

An effort has been made in the translation to preserve the sentence structure of the original, but not the punctuation, which has been revised in accordance with modern usage. Quotations from the Bible have normally been cited in the Douai version, with revisions to fit the text of the *Libellus*, as when it has *cara* in place of *onera* in Numbers 7: 9,[1] and occasionally with slight adjustments in order to avoid an excessive confusion of quotation marks.

[1] p. 62 (chap. 34).

LIBELLUS DE DIVERSIS ORDINIBUS

LIBELLUS DE DIVERSIS ORDINIBUS ET PROFESSIONIBUS QUI SUNT IN AECCLESIA

DILECTISSIMO fratri suo .R. unica dilectione sibi coniunctus frater .R. uiam Dei bene ac fidenter ut coepit tenere, in qua alius sic, alius sic ambulat.

Cum ab initio surgentis aecclesiae diuersi seruorum Dei profectus, diuersique extiterint professionum status, et maxime nostris temporibus diuersa monachorum canonicorumue surgat institutio in habitu uel cultu, ostendendum est Deo auxiliante, quae in talibus Dei seruis differentia, quae intentionis sit in diuersis professionibus forma. Ad demonstrandum ergo quod istae diuersitates professionum Deo placeant accingor, primo loco sermonem habiturus de diuersis ordinibus et professionibus monachorum et canonicorum, uel aliorum, secundo de habitu diuerso, tercio de epulis, quarto de labore manuum. Neminem uero moueat, quod ordinem professionum aliquantulum mutatum[a] inueniet. Nam pro certo scio canonicos monachosque maiorem locum in aecclesia tenere, et tamen neutrum horum primum positum reperiet. Ne enim dicatur de me quod in hoc opere quaeram quod meum est, meque honorare uelim, ideo canonicos primo loco non ponam. At uero nec monachos primo loco ponendos putaui, ne quis canonicorum conqueratur, quod qui in initio primitiuae aecclesiae primi ad opus Dei et testimonium Iesu esse meruerunt, primi ante monachos qui postea esse coeperunt positi non sint. Ideo ergo ita de ordinibus et professionibus tractare disposui, ut heremitae qui pauciores sunt et aliquando soli habitant primi ponerentur, sicut cum numeramus facere solemus, ut ab uno ad plures numerus surgat, et multiplicato numero, computator ad unum redeat. Verbi gratia cum ad centum uenerit, si quid numeret adhuc inuenerit, rursum ab uno numerare incipit. Ita et hic faciemus, primum heremitas ponentes, qui pauciores sunt et soli sepe habitant, deinde monachos, quorum multiplicior est numerus, sicque ad canonicos ueniemus, quorum maxima in

[a] mutatum *add. in marg.*

THE ORDERS AND CALLINGS OF
THE CHURCH

To his most beloved brother R. brother R. sends this, bound to him by extraordinary love, hoping he will hold well and faithfully to the way of God in which he began, and in which some walk one way and others another.

Since different servants of God have arisen from the beginning of the early church, and many kinds of callings have come into being, and particularly in our day, institutions of monks and canons differing in habit and worship are increasing, it is necessary to show, with God's help, how such servants of God differ and what the purposes of the different forms of callings are. So I undertake to show that these differences among the callings please God. First, the different orders and callings of monks, canons, and others must be discussed, second their different habits, third their diet, and fourth manual labour: and let no one be disturbed if he finds the arrangement of the orders somewhat changed. For I know certainly that monks and canons have the major place in the church and yet neither of them is accorded first place. And lest it be said of me that in this work I seek my own and desire to honour it, I shall not put the canons in first place. And indeed I have not thought of putting the monks in first place, lest any of the canons should complain that, although in the beginning of the primitive church they were found worthy of being first in God's service and in bearing witness to Jesus, they have not been put first before the monks, who came into existence later. Therefore I have decided to deal with the orders and callings in such a way that the hermits, who are fewer in number and usually live alone, are placed first, just as we are used to doing with numerals with the digits rising from one to many, and with the calculator returning to number one after he has reached a high number, as for example when he reaches a hundred he begins to count from one again if he finds he has more to count. And so we shall do likewise, putting the hermits first, who are fewer and often live alone, then the monks, whose numbers are greater, and we shall thus come to the canons, who

diuersis locis et frequens habitatio diuerse uiuentium esse comprobatur. Deinde, rursum incipientes ab inclusis, et ab his qui continenter uiuunt, et nec canonici nec monachi nec heremitae nec inclusi sed deicolae uel licoisi, id est, quasi legis custodes[a] possunt dici, itidem reuertemur ad mulieres quae heremiticam uitam ducunt, ascendentes ad sanctimonialium sanctitatem, necnon et ad illas quae cum sanctis et sub sanctis uiris iugum Christi suaue suscipiunt. Ad ultimum uero pene[b] ad inclusas et mulieres deicolas quas licoisas, id est, legis custodes uel[c] nichoisas uulgo uocamus, quasi sanctum Nycholaum imitantes ordinem professionum terminabimus, ut postea de habitu et epulis et labore manuum liberius pertractemus.[1] Postea autem subiungam de diuersis aecclesiarum consuetudinibus, ostendere cupiens in aecclesia Dei nichil agi ex consuetudine, quod ipsi conditori et capiti aecclesiae non placeat. Igitur dominum Deum nostrum conditorem omnium rogamus et petimus, et te ut roges precamur, quatinus nos de institutione seruorum suorum loquuturos adiuuet, ut eorum uitam imitando, ad sanctorum societatem pertingere quandoque ualeamus. Valeat in Christo dilectio tua frater karissime.

Incipit libellus de diuersis ordinibus et professionibus qui sunt in aecclesia.

I. *De heremitis qui sepe soli uel cum paucis habitant.*

1 De diuersis ordinibus uel professionibus sermonem habituri quae a religiosis uiris seculi pompam fugientibus in aecclesia Deo tenenda uouentur, primum oportet ostendere, quod etiam prima aetas Dei seruitium et cultum libens frequentauit. Ibi enim Abel

---

[a] uel . . . custodes *add. in marg.*   [b] pene *add. supra*   [c] licoisas . . .
custodes *add. in marg.*, uel *add. supra*

are known mainly to live in different kinds of places and to frequent different kinds of houses. Then again, beginning with the enclosed religious and with those who live chastely, and who are neither canons, nor monks, nor hermits, nor recluses, but are worshippers of God, or *licoisi*, that is, people who can be called, as it were, guardians of the law. Then similarly we shall revert to women, who lead an eremitical life, rising to the holiness of nuns, and to those who sweetly take up Christ's yoke with holy men or under their guidance. Last, however, we shall finish by just touching on the recluses and women who worship God, whom we call *licoisae*, that is, guardians of the law, or in the vernacular *nichoisae*, as if they were imitators of St. Nicholas, and after that we shall treat of the manner of life, diet, and manual labour more fully.[1] Later I shall add something about the different customs of the church, in the desire to show that nothing is done customarily in God's church which is displeasing to its Founder and Head. We beg and beseech our Lord God, therefore, and pray that you too beseech Him, that He will aid us for as long as we are to speak of the institutions of God's servants, so that by imitating their lives we shall be worthy some day of attaining the company of the saints. Farewell in Christ, most beloved brother.

Here begins the book on the various orders and callings of the church.

I. *Hermits, who usually live alone or with a few others.*

1 When speaking of the various orders and callings, in which religious men have taken vows, having fled the pomps of the world to worship God in the church, it is first necessary to show what was gladly practised once in the first age in the service and worship of God. Then indeed Abel offered worthy sacrifice,

---

[1] The derivation and the precise meaning of the terms *licoisi* and *nichoisae* is uncertain. The former appears only in marginal additions, but it is used in both the masculine and feminine forms, and the spelling is clear. G. G. Meersseman,'I penitenti nei secoli XI e XII', in *I laici*, p. 337 n. 134, suggested that they should be corrected to *le[g]icolae* and *nicolisae* respectively, since the author said that they referred to keepers of the law and imitators of St. Nicholas. But the manner in which the *nichoisae* resembled St. Nicholas is not clear. The author uses both terms in a favourable sense, and *nichoisae* carries none of the pejorative implications usually associated with the term *nicolaita* in the Middle Ages.

sacrificium acceptabile optulit, Seth nomen Dei cum sua progenie
inuocauit, Noe quoque in sua generatione iustus inuentus et ad
obaediendum Deo promptus ipso iubente archam fabricauit.
Vnde quia ad heremitas principium sermonis facere disposuimus,
intueamur si forte in primis hominibus aliquam horum seruorum
Dei similitudinem inuenire potuerimus. Nam illos priores homines
aliquando solos habitasse, eo indicio perdocemur quod Cain
occiso fratre suo Abel primus legitur ciuitatem aedificasse, et ex
nomine filii sui Enos eandem appellasse. Testatur etiam Iosephus
hoc ideo eum fecisse, quod latrocinia exerceret, et ad eadem secum
agenda familiares suos domesticosque intra muros conuenire
cogeret.[1] Vnde constat primam illam aetatem licet paruo tempore
multum innocenter uixisse, quibus nec aedificandarum domorum
adhuc cura erat, nec cibi potusque quanta nunc est diligentia, nec
uestium uanitas, nec auri argentique tanta acquirendi sollertia.
Graminibus enim et aqua simplici et arborum fructibus uti
Deus dixerat utebantur. Vnde et quidam facundissimus noster
phylosophus laudem primorum hominum carmine mirifico
decantans, ait: 'Felix nimium prior aetas, contenta fidelibus
aruis, nec inerti perdita luxu, facili quae sera solebat ieiunia
soluere glande. Non bachica munera norat, liquido confundere
melle. Nec lucida uellera[a] serum, tyrio miscere ueneno. Somnos
dabat herba salubres. Potum quoque lubricus annis, umbras alt-
issima pinus. Nondum maris alta secabant, nec mercibus undique
lectis, noua littora uiderat hospes.' Ad ultimum uero carminis huius,
idem subinfert: 'Heu primus quis fuit ille, auri qui pondera tecti,
2 gemmasque latere uolentes, preciosa pericula fodit?'[2] Si igitur
conceditur michi priores homines solos sepius habitasse, quia nec
in Genesi ante Cain quisquam uel ciuitatem uel domum legitur
construxisse, et Iosephus similiter ob rapinam fratricidae illius

---

[a] uellere *corr.* uellera

Seth called on God's name with his children, Noah was found just in his generation and, ready in obeying God, built the ark at His command. And since we have decided to start with hermits, let us consider whether perhaps we can find a likeness of these servants of God among the first men. Now we are clearly taught that the first men once lived alone by the fact that Cain, having killed his brother Abel, is the first who is said to have built a city and to have named it after his son Henoch. Josephus also writes that he did this, that he carried out robberies, and that for this purpose he made his friends and servants gather together within walls.[1] From this it is certain that in that first age men lived very innocently, even if only for a short time, having as yet no need to build houses, nor to worry about food and drink as much as is done now, nor about the vanity of clothing, nor about such skill in acquiring gold and silver. They used grass and water simply and the fruits of the trees, as God had said. So one of our most eloquent philosophers says, singing the praises of the first men in a wonderful song:

> Too much the former age was blest,
> When fields their pleased owners failed not,
> Who, with no slothful lust oppressed,
> Broke their long fasts with acorns eas'ly got.
> No wine with honey mixed was,
> Nor did they silk in purple colours steep;
> They slept upon the wholesome grass,
> And their cool drink did fetch from rivers deep.
> The pines did hide them with their shade,
> No merchants through the dangerous billows went,
> Nor with desire of gainful trade
> Their traffic into foreign countries sent.

At the end of this song he adds:

> Ah, who was he that first did show
> The heaps of treasure which the earth did hide,
> And jewels which lay close below,
> By which he costly dangers did provide?[2]

If therefore it is allowed me that the first men usually lived alone, since in Genesis we do not read that anyone before Cain built a house or a city, and Josephus testifies similarly, that they were

---

[1] Flavius Josephus, *Antiq. Jud.*, 1. 2. 2.

[2] Boethius, *Consol.*, ii metr. 5 (*CC*, xciv. 28-9; tr. H. F. Stewart and E K. Rand [Loeb Library], pp. 205-7).

haec adinuenta testatur, et phylosophi illius carmen illos in umbra arborum morasse decantat, sine luxu, sine cupiditate illa et iactantia quae modo in nobis est[a] uiuentes, et gramina ad usum uitae ut animantibus ita et hominibus a Deo sunt tradita, constat eosdem priores homines aliquam heremitarum similitudinem habuisse, quasi aliquem forte certum locum tenebant, uel ut homines aliquando se inuisebant, tamen de aedificiis uel uestibus cibo uel potu uel pecunia non magnopere curabant. Locum uero certum eos nequaquam tenuisse eo modo conitio, quia non ante Cain domus uel ciuitas aedificata fuit, et Iosephus eundem metas terris et limites primum imposuisse asserit.[1] Domorum ergo aedificandarum cura heremitis summa non conuenit, ne dicatur de eis quia heremum non incolunt, sed in heremo domos ciuitatum inuehere gestiunt. Vestis uilis, cibus grossior, potus permodicus, talibus congruit. Exercitatio corporalis,[2] ieiunia et uigiliae, illos gloriosos reddunt. Heremitae ergo nomen incassum non teneant, sed opere exornent. Habemus ergo in priori aetate heremitarum similitudinem expressam, ubi inuenimus Abel iustum in arborum umbra morantem et pascuis ouium intentum sine dubio solitudinem quaesisse, ubi et sine tumultu uiueret, et oues suae innocentiae indices nutriret, ac deinde de eisdem ouibus fructus capiens Domino offerret. Iustum enim erat, ut quia adhuc hominum paucitas erat, ille quem iustum Dominus uocare dignatus est solus Domino militaret, et quodammodo uitam solitariam oues animal sine dubio quietis amicum pascendo institueret. Vnde autem a Domino iustus appellatur? Quia oues pauit? Non. Sed quia cum oues pasceret, studuit ut Deo placeret. Nam et illi pastores Israel secundum Ezechiel prophetiam oues pascere uidebantur, de quorum manibus oues suas Dominus se requisiturum esse quia eas non pascerent sed se ipsos Dominus terribiliter interminatur.[3] Non igitur inde placuit Deo. Congruum profecto et aptum dico esse solitariae uitae pascendarum ouium opus, ubi et quies potest esse summa, et utilitas fructuum est maxima. Nam si bene inspicias, quid in oue ab utilitate uacuum? Si uellus attendas, ipsum uestit. Si pellem consideres, ipsa multis modis

---

[a] est *add. supra*

devised to further the robberies of that fratricide, and the song of this philosopher sings of their living in the shade of trees, without luxury, living without that covetousness and ostentation, which we now have, and using grass for the needs of their lives, as has been taught by God to men and animals—then it is evident that these first men were somewhat like hermits, in that they probably stayed in the same place, and even if men sometimes came to see them, they nevertheless gave little thought to buildings or clothes, food or drink or money. I do not think they ever stayed in a fixed place at that time, since no house or city was built before Cain. And Josephus claims him to be the first to set boundaries and limits on the earth.[1] It is therefore highly unsuitable for hermits to worry about the building of houses, lest it be said of them that they do not live in the desert, but desire to bring city-houses into the desert; coarse clothing, rougher food, and little drink is more suitable for such men. Bodily exercise,[2] fasts, and vigils confer glory on them. Thus they do not bear the name of hermit idly but embellish it with works. We find therefore a distinct likeness to hermits in the first age, when we find the just Abel living in the shade of trees and intent on grazing his sheep, having doubtless sought solitude, where he can both live without being disturbed and feed the sheep, which are the signs of his innocence, and then taking the offspring of these sheep make an offering to God. For it was right that because there were few men at that time, he whom God deemed worthy to call just should serve God alone and should, as it were, establish the solitary life by grazing sheep, an animal which is, no doubt, a lover of quietness. But why is he called just by the Lord? Because he grazed his sheep? No, but because while he grazed his sheep he was eager to please God. For those pastors of Israel, according to Ezechiel the prophet, seemed to graze sheep, and God says He will require His sheep from their hands: because they did not feed them but themselves instead, God threatened them in a terrible way.[3] He did not therefore please God by this. It is certainly apt and fitting for me to liken the solitary life to the work of grazing sheep, where quiet can be at its greatest and the usefulness of its fruits the highest. For if you consider well, what is there in a sheep that is not useful? Consider its fleece, it provides clothing. Consider its skin, it has many uses. Consider the meat, it provides

3

---

[1] Josephus, loc. cit.   [2] 1 Tim. 4: 8.   [3] Ezech. 34: 10.

prodest. Si carnem inspicias, ipsa pascit. Si lac cogites, paruulos
alit, maiores nichilominus delectat. Sed et illud quod deterius
esse putatur, uide quam utillimum agriculturae sit, ita ut arens
terra[1] stercoris eius fomento pinguescat. Talia ergo pecora curans
theoriam amplectebatur.[2] Videns enim cotidie gregem suum
multiplicari, amplificationem ouilis ad cordis latitudinem trahebat,
et sicut illi greges numero ampliabantur, sic in eo uirtutum
numerositas augmentabatur. Quas putas laudes in corde suo
Domino reddebat, cum nullus ei tumultus adesset, et profectus
uirtutum simul et gregum numquam illi deesset. Credo nec ipsum
balatum pecorum contempnebat, sed secundum hunc mortalitatis
huius erumpnam deflebat, profecto socius illius, qui ait: 'Infelix
ego homo, quis me liberabit de corpore mortis huius?'[3] Intueor
etiam quodammodo solitariam uitam eum dilexisse, qui et artem
diuersam ab arte fratris pessimi quesiuit, et qui coniugii copulam
non curauit. Nam ut credo nullus usque ad Noe in cathalogo
generationis humanae nominatur, preter hunc sine uxore uixisse
ut profecto ignotesceret, quia solitarium hominem oportet sine
uxore quae Domini sunt[4] quomodo Domino placeat cogitare.

4 Age ergo quisquis solitariam uitam amas, et ab illo qui primus
iustus appellatus est, exemplum et boni incrementum operis
accipe. Inspice etiam si alicubi noster Iesus huic uitae simile quid
egerit.[5] Scriptum est de eo in euangelio Iohannis:[a] 'Iesus uero
cum cognouisset quia uenturi erant ut raperent eum et facerent
sibi regem, fugit in montem ipse solus.'[6] Ecce Iesus meus solus
in montem secedit, ne heremita dubitaret montana uel heremum
solus habitare. Si ergo dominus Iesus sicut et ante nos sepe
dictum est legendo in libro Ysaiae intra sinagogam lector, et

---

[a] in . . . Iohannis *add. supra*

food. Consider the milk, it nourishes infants and still delights adults. But even that which might be thought worthless, consider how useful it is to husbandry, so that dry land[1] is enriched by the fomentation of its dung. Thus the care of such flocks included contemplation.[2] Seeing his herd multiply day by day he likened the increase in his sheep to an enlargement of his heart, and just as those flocks grew in number so did the legion of his virtues increase. What praises did he render, do you think, to God in his heart, with nothing present to disturb him and a constant growth of virtues and of flocks never failing? I do not believe that he despised even the bleating of his sheep, but wept over the anguish of our mortality like them, a sympathizer indeed with him who says: 'Unhappy man that I am, who shall deliver me from the body of this death?'[3] I also somehow perceive that he loved his solitary life, he who had sought out a way of life different from that of his wicked brother and had given no thought to conjugal embraces. For I believe that up to Noah no one else is named in the list of the human race who lived without a wife, so that it should be known clearly that a solitary man should live without a wife, meditating on the things which are of God[4] and how he should please God. Come then, whoever you are that love the solitary life, and take an example from him who was the first to be called just, and receive an increase of good works. See also whether our Jesus did anything that could be compared to this kind of life.[5] It is written of Him in St. John's Gospel: 'Jesus therefore, when he knew that they would come to take him by force and make him king, fled again into the mountain, himself alone.'[6] Behold my Jesus withdrawing alone into the mountain, lest the hermit should doubt whether he should live alone in the mountains or the wilderness. If therefore the Lord Jesus, as has often previously been said, was a lector by His reading of Isaiah

4

---

[1] Josh. 15: 19.

[2] On the use of the term *theoria* in medieval monastic sources, see Louis Gougaud, 'La *Theoria* dans la spiritualité médiévale', *Revue d'ascétique et de mystique*, iii (1922), 381–94, and Leclercq, *Vocabulaire*, pp. 80–144.

[3] Rom. 7: 24.   [4] Phil. 2: 21.

[5] On the theme of the example set for monks by Christ's fighting the Devil in solitude (referred to here and pp. 52–4 below), see Jean Becquet, 'La règle de Grandmont', *Bulletin de la Société archéologique et historique du Limousin*, lxxxvii (1958), 20 n. 36, referring among other examples to the rule of Stephen of Grandmont, cap. XLVI (*PL*, cciv. 1154B).

[6] John 6: 15.

eliminando de templo nummularios hostiarius, et eiciendo demones exorcista, et illuminando cecos ceroferarius, et ministrando
subdiaconus, et predicando euangelium regni leuita, et se ipsum
offerendo sacerdos, non erit absurdum si secedendo in montem
uel in desertum quod heremitarum est proprium, uitam eorum
in se ipso consecrasse dicatur.[1] Sic debent et illi quibus pro bonis
operibus mundus arridet facere, si sese metiendo cognouerint
sine iactantiae peccato inter homines non posse bona opera facere.
Habes et in Marco scriptum, quia cum mundasset leprosum, et
dixisset ei, 'uide nemini dixeris',[2] ille egressus coepit predicare et
diffamare sermonem, ita ut non posset manifeste in ciuitatem
introire, sed foris in desertis locis esse. Num ergo timebat Iesus
boni operis iactantiam? Non. Sed ostendebat nobis humanam
debere uitare laudem. Video etiam dominum Iesum pene omnium
professionum aecclesiasticarum similitudinem in se ipso demon-
strasse, quod etiam pro posse suis locis ostendemus, cum de aliis
professionibus sermonem texuerimus. Habes ergo in prima aetate
Abel pastorem ouium per solitudinem Deo placentem, et ob
hoc eius suscepta munera, habes et in secunda aetate patriarchas
pascuis ouium intentos, et cum suis gregibus id est cum sua
simplicitate, hac atque illac terrenos homines fugientes. Habes et
Moysen solum gregem pascentem in desertis Syna uel Choreb[a]
(Vt Ieronimus dicit iunguntur sibi Syna et Choreb, et unum
sunt.)[b][3] Domini uidisse gloriam. Inspice etiam post datam legem
Heliam et multos alios per solitudinem Deo placuisse, accipe
etiam gratanter dominum meum Iesum in montem uel in desertum
fugisse, et habebis ante te quos imitari possis. Tempore uero
reuelatae gratiae nosti, quam frequentata sit solitudinum habitatio.
Quod si forte ignoras, lege Antonii et Pauli et aliorum hystorias,
5 ut possis agnoscere. Sed dicit aliquis: Quid audes dicere, quod
ante te nullus ausus est asserere? Quis umquam Abel et patriarchas
Moysenque et rursum Dominum heremitis assimilauit? Ad quod
respondeo me non alicui melius sapienti et intelligenti preiudicare,

---

[a] uel Choreb *add. supra*   [b] Vt Ieronimus . . . sunt. *add. in marg.*

in the synagogue, was a door-keeper by His driving the money-lenders from the temple, was an exorcist by casting out demons, was a candle-bearer by giving sight to the blind, was a sub-deacon by ministering, a levite by preaching the Gospel of His reign, and a priest by offering Himself, it will not be absurd to say that by withdrawing into the mountain or the desert, as is proper for hermits, He consecrated their life in Himself.[1] Those whom the world praises for their good works should do likewise, if they have discovered by self-examination that they cannot do good works among men without the sin of vainglory. For you find it written in Mark that when He had cleansed the leper and said to him: 'See thou tell no one',[2] the leper being gone out began to publish and blaze abroad the word, so that He could not openly go into the city but was without in desert places. Now did Jesus fear that He would be vainglorious about His good works? No, but He showed us we must avoid human praise. I see that Jesus demonstrated in Himself the likeness of almost all the callings of the church, which we shall show in their place as well as we can, when we come to speak of the other callings. You have therefore in the first age Abel the shepherd of his sheep, pleasing God by solitude and receiving his reward for this; you have in the second age the patriarchs too, intent on grazing their sheep, and fleeing here and there from earthly men, with their flocks, that is their simplicity. You have also Moses seeing the glory of God in the desert of Sinai or Horeb (as Jerome says, Sinai and Horeb are adjoining and make one),[3] alone and grazing his sheep. You can see also, after the giving of the law to Elias, many others pleasing God by solitude. Accept joyfully then my lord Jesus, who fled into the mountain or the desert, and you will have before you examples you can imitate. But in the time of revealed grace you already know how frequented are the habitations of solitude. And if you are perhaps ignorant of this, read the stories of Anthony
5 and Paul and others so that you may know them. But someone will say: How dare you assert what no one has ever had the courage to say before you? Who ever has compared Abel and the patriarchs and Moses and even the Lord to hermits? To which I reply: I do not judge myself better in wisdom and understanding

---

[1] On the ordinal of Christ and the sacramental grades listed here and p. 60 below, see introd., p. xxi.

[2] Mark 1: 44.   [3] Jerome, *Loc. heb.* (PL, xxiii. 935B).

sed meliora dicentem paratum audire. Sed qui optima dicere ob ingenii mei tenuitatem fortasse nescio, ideo semper tacebo? Qui aurum non habeo, quod possum facio, in domo Dei uel pilos caprarum[1] offero. Protegunt enim et ipsi ornaturam diuini tabernaculi, et utiles sunt in domo Domini. Fidenter etiam dico salua fide et pace christiana, non multum abhorrere a uero, si illum heremitis assimilem qui forte heremitae nomen[a] non habuit, ideo quia forsitan adhuc inuentum non erat, et heremiticam uitam optime tenuit. Non multum contendo de nomine, ubi operis uideo effectum. Nam sine hoc nomine potest eiusdem uitae fructus acquiri, sine uita uero solum nomen inane est. Participem ergo te constitue non tantum nominis sed etiam uitae heremiticae et perfectum sectatorem quisquis eam aggressus es, et humilis factus cum euangelico agricola cophino stercoris terram cordis tui ne sit tanquam ficulnea infructuosa humectare et pinguescere per paenitentiam facito. Postea uero tanquam 'paruulus in Christo lac'[2] humanitatis eius ut nutriaris accipe, et sic 'iusticiam quae ex fide est'[3] tanquam ouium uellus indue, pellem quoque eius id est, mortalitatem quam pro te Iesus assumpsit, ad omnia utilia tibi detrahe, ut ad extremum carnem eius et sanguinem quae uere sunt cibus et potus digne sumens tuum 'quod mortale est absorbeatur a uita',[4] ut 'cum Christus apparuerit uita nostra, appareas cum ipso in gloria'.[5] Haec autem omnia obseruans, uide ne alterius ordinis hominem de suo proposito uel professione reprehendas, etiam si leuioris uitae sit, ne 'dilatans philacteria tua et magnificans' cum Phariseis 'fimbrias',[6] Deus ad te ueniens partem tuam cum hypochritis ponat. Ama ergo in alio quod ipse non habes, ut amet alius in te quod ipse non habet, ut utriusque sit bonum quod uterque fecerit, et coniungantur amore qui disiunguntur opere, et fiat unusquisque cum apostolo 'omnibus omnia',[7] ut perueniatis nobiscum ad eum qui est 'omnia in omnibus'.[8] Caeterum non moueat quemquam si in hoc ordine quaedam diuersitas appareat, et aliter

6

---

[a] nomen *add. supra*

than anyone else, but am ready to listen to anyone who speaks better. But perhaps because I do not know how to say the best things, through dullness of wit, must I therefore always keep silence? Having no gold, what can I do in the Lord's house but offer a cloth of goats' hair?[1] They protect the furnishings of the divine tabernacle and are useful in the Lord's house. For I say sincerely, saving the Christian faith and peace, that it is not a great departure from the truth if I compare to the hermits one who perhaps did not have the name of hermit, perhaps because it had not yet been invented, and who held to the eremitical life perfectly. I do not argue much about the name when I see the works performed, for the fruits of that life can be acquired without the name, but without the life the name alone is empty. Make yourself then a sharer not only in the name but also in the life of a hermit, and whoever has become a perfect practitioner in it and has become humble, may you do penance and water and fertilize, with the husbandry of the Gospel as the basket of dung, the soil of your heart, lest it be like the barren fig tree. Afterwards take as 'a little one in Christ the milk'[2] of His humanity for your nourishment; clothe yourself in the sheep's fleece, that is in 'the justice that is of faith',[3] and in its skin too, that is the mortality which Jesus took on for you; take everything useful to you, so that at the end, consuming worthily His flesh and blood, which are truly food and drink, 'that which is mortal' of you 'may be swallowed up by life',[4] so that 'when Christ who is our life shall appear, you shall appear with Him in glory'.[5] Observing all this, beware lest you reprove men of a different order for their discipline or calling, even if it is easier, lest 'making your phylacteries broad and enlarging your fringes'[6] with the Pharisees you be placed by God when He comes to you among the hypocrites. Love in others what you yourself do not have, so that another shall love in you what he does not have, so that what either does shall be good for the other and those shall be joined in love who are separate in works, and let each be, with the apostle, 'all things to all men',[7] so that you shall attain with us to Him who is 'all in all'.[8] Let no one else be disturbed if a certain diversity should appear in this order and each arranges his life

[1] Exod. 25:4; 35: 6, etc.   [2] 1 Cor. 3: 1–2.   [3] Rom. 9: 30.
[4] 2 Cor. 5: 4.   [5] Col. 3: 4.   [6] Matt. 23: 5.
[7] 1 Cor. 9: 22.   [8] 1 Cor. 15: 28; Col. 3: 11.

atque aliter unusquisque uitam suam instituat, ueluti est illud,
ut quidam horum soli habitent, quidam uero adiunctis sibi duobus
aut tribus aut pluribus, et illud quod alter altero leuius aut durius
uiuit, cum et hanc diuersitatem in antiquis heremitis inueniamus,
et unusquisque arbitrii sui potestate utatur, ut quantumlibet, et
quantum uires suas pensat aggrediatur, nec a Domino inde damp-
7 netur.[1] Si autem aliquando contigerit ut aliquis hanc institutionem
aggressus non multum sibi utilem esse perspexerit, si aliam rursus
assumat, non inde debet iudicari licet hoc leuitate nimia aliquando
contingat, nisi forte priorem illam institutionem se obseruaturum
uouerit, cum et arboris plantam in uno loco infructuosam et
inutilem manere uideamus, quae mota de loco crescit et frondescit,
et fructus in altum attollit. Si autem adhuc tibi displicet quod
omnes huius professionis homines non uno modo uiuunt, inspice
facturam mundi a bono conditore diuerse dispositam, et de diuersis
concordem effecisse armoniam, ut caelum superius, terra inferius,
aqua grauior, aer leuior, homo belua sapientior, unum supra,
alterum infra positum sit, et non miraberis si etiam in seruis
Dei alter alteri preferatur, cum secundum euangelium 'in domo
patris mansiones multae sint',[2] et secundum beatum Augustinum
'mansionem' illic 'pro suo quisque accepturus est merito'.[3] Placet
ergo Deo ista in seruis suis uitae diuersitas, nec debet dicere lutum
figulo[a] quare 'sic me' uel illum 'fecisti, quia habet figulus potestatem facere ex eadem massa aliud uas in honorem aliud in con-
tumeliam',[4] et 'in domo magna sunt uasa non solum aurea et
argentea, sed et lignea et fictilia',[5] et utraque ad opus domus utilia.
Esto ergo uas utile et electum in domo Dei tui,[6] ne propter in-
credulitatem et fratris detractionem frangaris, et tanquam testa
de uase fictili habeas unde tangentem mordeas, et non habeas
unde in te missa conserues. Lauda ex opere artificem, ex creatura
creatorem, ut si forte ipsa[b] assequi non uales quae alius habet,
amando tamen in alio cum eo premia uitae caelestis assequaris.

differently, with some living alone, some with two or three or
more, living a life that is easier for some and harder for others,
with a diversity such as we find among the hermits of old, and
let each use the judgement and strength he has so that he may
attempt as much as he wishes and as much as his powers allow,
7 and not be condemned by the Lord for it.[1] If, however, it should
some time happen that a man having joined this institution should
not find it of much use to him and joins another, he must not be
judged on this account, though this light-mindedness occurs too
often, unless he has vowed himself to remain with this first
institution, for it is as with a tree planted in barren soil and
remaining there uselessly, which transplanted grows and puts
out leaves and bears fruit on high. If it still displeases you that
all men of this calling do not live in the same way, look at the
creation fashioned by the good Creator in various ways, and how
a harmony has been achieved from different chords, so that the
heavens are placed above, the earth below, water made heavier,
air lighter, man wiser than the beasts, one above and another
below, and you will not wonder if even in God's service different
things are preferred, for according to the Gospel: 'In my Father's
house there are many mansions.'[2] According to the blessed
Augustine, 'Everyone will receive in heaven a mansion according
to his merit.'[3] This diversity of life in His service is pleasing to
God, nor should the clay say to the potter: 'Why hast thou made
me this or that?' since 'the potter hath power over the clay, of the
same lump, to make one vessel unto honour and another unto
dishonour',[4] and 'in the house there are great vessels, not only of
gold and silver, but of wood and earthenware too',[5] and each is
useful for the work of the house. Be therefore a profitable and
chosen vessel in the house of your God,[6] lest through lack of faith
and slander of your brothers you break into pieces, and like a
sherd from the earthen vessel you have a biting edge and have
nothing to contain what has been put into you. Praise the Maker
from His work, the Creator from His creatures, so that if you are
perhaps unable to attain what another has, you will attain, by loving
it in another, to the prize of heavenly life with him.

---

[1] On the theme of diversity within unity used here and below, see introd., p. xxv.
[2] John 14: 2.
[3] Augustine, *Tract. in Ioh.*, 7 (*CC*, xxxvi. 495).
[4] Rom. 9: 20-1.   [5] 2 Tim. 2: 20.   [6] 2 Tim. 2: 21.

II. *De monachis qui iuxta homines habitant, sicut Cluniacenses et eorum similes.*

8 Nunc ad illos noster sermo dirigatur,[1] qui monachi nomen proprie obtinent, quorum alii a turbis omnino seggregati, uitam Deo placabilem ieiuniis et orationibus et corporali exercitatione ducunt, alii iuxta homines in ciuitatibus et castellis et uillis positi, de elemosinis fidelium et reditibus aecclesiarum decimisque sustentantur, soli theoriae operam dantes, et 'primum quaerentes regnum Dei', sperantes quod necessaria huius uitae licet ea non quaerant

9 'adicientur eis'.[2] De ipso autem nomine monachi pauca dicamus.[3] Nomen istud unum uel solum sonat. Quid ergo dicet aliquis a nomine et actu sibi uult tanta diuersitas? Si ergo monachus unus uel solus intelligitur, quare omnes aut pene omnes monachi gregatim habitant? Ad quod respondeo, quia ille unus et solus recte dicitur, qui unum et solum cum fratribus uiuendi habet affectum, et a uoluptate secularium omnino seggregatum. Sed forte hoc concedatur, de his qui longe se constituerunt a turbis. Si autem mouet aliquem quomodo hi qui in ciuitatibus degunt, hoc nomen optinere possint, cum pater Ieronimus dicat, monachum solitudo facit non publicum,[4] respondeo nullum monachum nec affectu nec societate secularibus debere coniungi. Licet enim inter homines aliquando contingat eos aedificia construere, tamen non perdit prerogatiuam nominis, si frater cum fratribus quorum bona et iocunda in unum habitantium[5] societas est secularia postponat, et blandientes sirenas in huius uitae pelago constitutus surda aure pertransiens horrescat. Tunc enim monachus uere unus et solus est, si cum fratribus unum sentiat, unum et solum Deum colat, et secundum Salomonem 'frater adiutus a fratre unam ciuitatem fortem'[6] dilectionem Dei scilicet et proximi in

10 corde suo constituat. Haec de monachi nomine dicta sint. Caeterum inspiciamus si alicubi in antiquis inuenire possimus harum institutionum exempla, et ostendere non recenter nec solum post mortem et resurrectionem Christi, sed etiam antiquitus istam

II. *Monks who live close to men, such as the Cluniacs and the like.*

8 Now our words are directed to those[1] who have the name of monk
in its strict sense, of whom some lead a life pleasing to God, away
from all disturbance, by fasting, prayer, and physical asceticism,
and some who, living among men in cities, towns, and villages,
are sustained by the alms of the faithful, church revenues, and
tithes, and who carry out only the work of contemplation, 'seeking
first the kingdom of God' and hoping that the necessities of life,
though they do not seek them, 'will be added unto them'.[2] We shall
9 say little of the name of monk itself.[3] The name means 'one' or
'alone'. Why then, someone will say, is there such a disparity
between the name and the actuality? If monk means 'one' or
'alone', why do all or nearly all monks live in groups? To which
I reply that he is rightly called 'one' and 'alone' who prefers
to live with his brothers and to be completely cut off from the
pleasures of the world. But perhaps this is allowed to those
who establish themselves at a distance from crowds. If it
should disturb someone that those who stay in cities should be
able to gain this name, and he should say with father Jerome:
'Solitude makes the monk, not public life',[4] I shall reply that
no monk may be concerned with worldly things either by state
of mind or by mixing in society. For though it may be necessary
for them to put up buildings in inhabited places sometimes, a
brother does not lose the privilege of the name, if he lives with
brothers whose company is good and agreeable, dwelling together
in unity,[5] disregards the world, and, fearing the alluring sirens
in the sea of this life, passes by resolutely with deaf ears. For then
the monk is indeed one and alone, if he feels one with his brothers,
worships the one and only God, and if, as Solomon says, 'a brother
that is helped by his brother' forms a 'strong city',[6] that is the
love of God and his neighbour in his heart. This is what I have
10 to say about the name of monk. Let us see whether we can find
anywhere in antiquity further examples of these institutions and
can point to a diversity of observances occurring not only recently,
not only since the death and resurrection of Christ, but also in

---

[1] Cf. Benedict, *Reg.*, Prol., 3.   [2] Matt. 6: 33; Luke 12: 31.
[3] On the following passage, cf. Leclercq, *Vocabulaire*, pp. 19–20, who called it
'une page dense et belle' citing 'toutes les données de la tradition'.
[4] Cf. Jerome, *Ep.* 14. 6 (*CSEL*, liv. 52) and *Ep.* 58. 5 (ibid. 533).
[5] Ps. 132: 1.   [6] Prov. 18: 19.

diuersitatum obseruantiam quae nostris temporibus in monachis
uiget esse percelebratam. Dicamus ergo de his qui[a] in ciuitatibus
uel castellis habitant, si quid horum simile in antiquis inueniamus.
Scriptum in libro Malachim primo[b] quod dixerit Samuhel ad
Saul postquam eum unxit in regem: 'Post haec uenies in collem
Domini, ubi est statio Phylistinorum. Et cum ingressus fueris ibi
urbem, obuium habebis gregem prophetarum descendentium
de excelso, et ante eos psalterium, et tympanum, et tibiam, et
cytharam, ipsosque prophetantes, et insiliet in te spiritus Domini,
et prophetabis cum eis, et mutaberis in uirum alium.'[1] Ecce
quomodo arridet uetusta hystoria modernis monachorum conuer-
sationibus. Ille enim in regnum sublimatus ad regendum populum
Dei, scilicet ut uitia extirparet et populum uirtutum nutriret et
tueretur, pro signo ei dicitur ut in collem Dei ueniat, qui collis
sicut Ieronimus testatur habitatio prophetarum erat,[2] quia decet
Christum Domini tales imitari, qui licet corpore sint in terra,
tamen super terram conuersatione se esse demonstrent,[3] quod
habitatione collis hoc loco non inconuenienter ostenditur. Quod
uero statio Phylistinorum ibi esse ostenditur ubi est habitatio
prophetarum, nostro intellectui fauet, quia decet et a turbis
seggregatos iuxta malignos et qui sunt 'cadentes uel ruina populi'[4]
quod interpretantur Phylistiim habitationem habere, ut 'aliis
odor uitae in uitam'[5] iuxta apostolum existentes cadant et ruant
ipsi[c] maligni a malicia sua interficientes et ruere facientes in
semetipsis populum peccatorum, et humiliati sanentur, 'aliis odor
mortis in mortem'[5] manentes persequutiones a filiis mortis
sustineant, ut ad purum per tribulationis ignem decocti, dicant
cum psalmista: 'Transiuimus per ignem et aquam, et eduxisti
nos in refrigerium.'[6] Sequitur etiam in lectione illa: 'Et cum
ingressus fueris ibi urbem, obuium habebis gregem prophetarum
descendentium de excelso.'[7] Intuere quoniam ipsi prophetae

---

[a] qui *add. supra*   [b] primo *add. supra*   [c] ipsi *add. supra*

antiquity, a diversity which in our day flourishes among monks. Let us speak therefore of those who live in cities and towns and see whether we can find anything like them in antiquity. It is written in the first book of Kings that Samuel said to Saul after he had joined him in the kingship: 'After that thou shalt come to the hill of the Lord, where the garrison of the Philistines is. And when thou shalt be come there into the city, thou shalt meet a company of prophets coming down from the high place, with a psaltery and a timbrel, and a pipe and a harp before them; and they shall be prophesying, and the spirit of the Lord shall come upon thee, and thou shalt prophesy with them and shalt be changed into another man.'[1] See how ancient history supports the way of life of modern monks. For it was said as a sign to him, who had been elevated to the kingship to rule God's people, that is to root out vices and nourish them in virtue and protect them, that he should come to the hill of God, which hill, as Jerome testifies, was the dwelling-place of the prophets,[2] because such men who, though in the body on earth, show in their conversation that they are above the earth,[3] and this is shown not inappropriately by their living on a hill, should imitate the anointed of the Lord. That the garrison of the Philistines is shown to be there, where the prophets live, favours our interpretation, since those who are segregated from the crowds should have a dwelling-place next to the wicked and those who are 'the downfall or ruin of the people',[4] which is the meaning of Philistine, in order that, being 'to some the odour of life unto life',[5] as the Apostle says, these wicked people may fall and tumble from their evil, killing and causing to be ruined in themselves the people of sin, and, humbled, may be cured, and in order that, being 'to others the odour of death unto death',[5] they may bear persecution from the sons of death, so that tempered by the pure fire of tribulation, they may say with the Psalmist: 'We have passed through fire and water: and thou hast brought us out into a refreshment.'[6] There follows in this lesson: 'And when thou shalt be come there into the city, thou shalt meet a company of prophets coming down from the high place.'[7]

[1] 1 Kgs. 10: 5–6.
[2] Ps.-Jerome, *In libros Regum* (*PL*, xxiii. 1336D).
[3] Cf. Phil. 3:20.
[4] Jerome, *Nom. heb.* (*CC*, lxxii. 66).
[5] 2 Cor. 2: 16.   [6] Ps. 65: 12.
[7] 1 Kgs. 10: 5.

et in excelso manebant, et aliquando de excelso descendebant,
et per ciuitatem transibant, et uide si non isto etiam tempore hoc
agitur, quando monachi qui in ciuitatibus habitant, aduenientes
quosque suscipiunt, ut donum Dei quod ipsi habent pro uiribus
aliis impendant. Vnde et descendere de excelso dicuntur, quia
infirmis compatiuntur, ut infirmis facti infirmi infirmos lucrentur.
Gregatim etiam ueniunt, ut ubi plures inueneris uitae unius
comites, quos etiam infirmos homines esse sicut te ipsum
nosti, non dubites cum eis uno spiritu participari. Dicitur etiam
ibi, quia 'ante eos psalterium et tympanum et tybia et cythara,
et ipsi prophetantes'.[1] Oportet enim tales homines semper
habere uerbum Dei, quod quasi psalterium de superioribus
resonat, et quod 'de caelo a regalibus sedibus'[2] uenit, et
super omnes est, habere et tympanum quod ex mortuis ani-
malibus sit, pelle detracta et siccata, ut immortalitatem quam
assequi cupiunt, bonis operibus consolidati et indurati resonent.
Conuenit etiam his tybia, quae ab uno surgit et in duo exten-
ditur, scilicet ut Deum diligant et proximum. Habent ante se
et cytharam quae ab inferioribus resonat, quia his omnibus
'mortificationem' Christi 'in corpore suo circumferre'[3] congruit.
Aliter enim spiritum sanctum assequi non ualent, nisi ista obseruauerint, nec aliquem de his qui regnum mortis in se destruere
cupiunt, et regnum uitae et iusticiae in se construere imitatorem
12 sui efficient. Dicitur etiam in illa scriptura, 'et insiliet in te
spiritus Domini, et prophetabis cum eis, et mutaberis in uirum
alium'.[4] Videns enim quilibet regni caelestis particeps et uocatione
diuina dignus,[5] seruos Dei ita uiuentes, accipit diuinum amorem,
et cum eis se in conuersatione iungens, narrat futuram electorum
gloriam, mutaturque in uirum alium, ut qui ante fuit blasphemus
et iniuriosus, nunc sit diuinae misericordiae predicator assiduus.
13 Sed dicet aliquis: Quare id quod etiam clericis et multis aliis
uel omnibus fidelibus congruere potest, monachis tantum qui in
ciuitatibus degunt assignas? Respondeo quidem omnibus 'christ-
ianis uirtutes animi et regnum uirtutum contra uitia et feruorem
spiritus sancti et susceptionem tanti doni congruere, sed in his

Understand that these prophets both remained in the high place and sometimes came down from it and went through the city. And see whether this is not also done in our day, when monks who live in cities also receive visitors so that they can use as much as they can for other men the gift of God which they have. For this reason they are said to come down from the high place, since they have compassion for the weak, so that weakened by the weak they convert them. They go in companies, so that when you find many companions in one life, who you know are weak men like yourself, you have no doubt that you are sharing in one spirit with them. It is also said there: 'With a psaltery and a timbrel and a pipe and a harp before them and they shall be prophesying.'[1] It is fitting that such men always have God's word, which sounds from above, like a psaltery, and which comes 'down from heaven from thy royal throne'[2] and is above all, that they have a timbrel also, which is made from the stripped and dried skins of dead animals, so that they should resound the immortality which they desire to attain, made firm and hard by good works. The pipe is also fitting for them, which rising in one piece then divides into two, meaning that they love God and their neighbour. They have also a harp before them, which resounds from below, since it is fitting for each of these people to 'bear in his body the mortification of Christ'.[3] Unless they have observed this, they cannot attain the Holy Spirit and will not make into an imitator of Him anyone who desires to destroy in himself the kingdom of death and construct in himself the kingdom of life and justice. It is also said in this part of Scripture: 'And the spirit of the Lord shall come upon thee, and thou shalt prophesy with them and shalt be changed into another man.'[4] Anyone sharing in the kingdom of heaven and worthy of the divine vocation,[5] seeing God's servants living in this way, accepts the divine love and, joining himself with them in a holy life, tells of the future glory of the chosen and is changed into another man, so that he who was before blasphemous and unjust is now a zealous preacher of divine mercy. But, someone will say, why do you assign to monks who live in cities what is more suitable for clerics and many other of the faithful? I answer that the virtues of the soul, the reign of virtue against vices, the ardour of the Holy Spirit and the acceptance of such gifts

---

[1] 1 Kgs. 10: 5.   [2] Wisd. 18: 15.   [3] 2 Cor. 4: 10.
[4] 1 Kgs. 10: 6.   [5] 2 Thess. 1: 11.

quae supradixi uideo quandam monachorum talium propriam assignationem. Nam ibi uideo collem Domini iuxta stationem Phylistinorum, inuenio et urbem, et in ipsa Dei seruos congregatos, et Deum laudantes, unde salua fide conitio eos seruos Dei qui in ciuitatibus degunt et monachi sunt, nec secularium sicut clerici et sacerdotes sed sui tantum curam habent prefigurari. Vnde talibus monachis cautum esse debere confirmo, quod in pluribus locis uideo, ut officinae talium ad habitationem hominum iuxta se positorum non respiciant, sed extra secularium habitationem intuitus suos defigant, ut ducti cum Iesu 'in desertum ab spiritu ut temptentur a diabolo',[1] si forte diabolus habitationem illam secularium ostenderit eis dicens, 'haec omnia uobis ad uoluptatem dabo, si procidentes a statu professionis uestrae adoraueritis me',[2] positi cum Moyse in deum Pharaonis id est illius dissipatoris, respondeant sibi non temptatori, o anima, 'dominum Deum tuum adorabis', non Sathanam.[3] Intuere adhuc dominum Iesum, si forte simile aliquid fecerit. Narrat euangelista Iohannes: 'Iesus autem' inquit, 'iam non palam ambulabat apud Iudeos, sed abiit in regionem iuxta desertum in ciuitatem quae dicitur Effrem, et ibi morabatur cum discipulis suis.'[4] Ecce habes Iesum proximum morti apud Iudeos occisores suos, iam non palam ambulantem, sed regionem deserto proximam quaerentem, et in ea cum discipulis manentem, et hoc in ciuitatem quae dicitur Effrem. Effrem interpretatur fertilis uel auctus ab augendo.[5] Vides quid in temptationibus suis in quibus et discipuli eius cum ipso manserunt sicut ipse perhibet, quaesierit Iesus. Quaesiuit enim et esuriuit et sitiuit salutem et augmentum seruorum suorum, et hoc iuxta desertum secundum propheticam uocem, 'scissae sunt in deserto aquae et torrentes in solitudine',[6] ut 'laetetur deserta et inuia, et germinans germinet',[7] 'et fructificet unum .xxx. et unum .LX. et unum centum'.[8] Tu uero qui

is fitting for all Christians, but in the matters I have written of above I see such an appropriate assignment for monks, for there I see the hill of the Lord next to the garrison of the Philistines, and I find the city and God's servants gathered together in it praising God. So I conjecture, saving the faith, that those servants of God who live in cities and are monks and do not have charge of secular men, like clerics and priests, but only of themselves, are prefigured there. And so I assert that such monks, as I see in many places, should be careful and not pay attention to the premises that are likely to be put up near the houses of men living next to them. They should fix their gaze beyond secular dwellings, so that with Jesus 'led by the spirit into the desert to be tempted by the devil',[1] if by chance the devil should show them that secular dwelling, saying: 'All these will I give you for your pleasure if, falling down from the standards of your vows, you will adore me',[2] placed with Moses before the god of Pharaoh, that is of his destroyer, they may reply to themselves not to their tempter: 'O soul, the Lord thy God shalt thou adore, not Satan.'[3] See again the Lord Jesus, whether he perhaps did something similar. John the Evangelist writes: 'Wherefore Jesus walked no more openly among the Jews; but he went into a country near the desert, unto a city that is called Ephrem. And there he abode with his disciples.'[4] There you have Jesus near His death not walking openly now among His Jewish murderers but seeking a desert region nearby and abiding there with His disciples, and this in the city called Ephrem. Ephrem means 'fertile' or 'growth', from growing.[5] You see what Jesus was seeking in His temptations in which His disciples stayed with Him, as He demonstrates. He sought and hungered and thirsted after salvation and a growth of His servants, and this near the desert, according to the voice of the prophet: 'For waters are broken out in the desert and streams in the wilderness'[6] in order that 'the land that was desolate and impassable shall be glad, and it shall bud forth and blossom'[7] 'and yield fruit, the one thirty, another sixty, and another a hundred'.[8] You who indeed have become a monk and under the

---

[1] Matt. 4: 1. [2] Cf. Matt. 4: 9.
[3] Matt. 4: 10. [4] John 11: 54.
[5] Jerome, *Nom. heb.* (*CC*, lxxii. 142). [6] Isa. 35: 6.
[7] Isa. 35: 1–2.
[8] Mark 4: 20. On the exegesis of the sower's fruits in Matt. 13: 8 and Mark 4: 20, see Antonio Quacquarelli, *Il triplice frutto della vita christiana: 100, 60 e*

monachus effectus es, et sub abbatis imperio quasi cum Iesu moraris, fuge ne ambules per uias terrae tenebrosas, sed auertendo faciem tuam a uiis seculi, et ab habitatione hominum quorum 'nouit Deus cogitationes quoniam uanae sunt',[1] esto in Effrem quaerens augeri et ampliari uirtutum multiplicitate et fratrum numerositate, ut bono exemplo tuo et conuersatione plurimi secularium conuertantur, et augeatur numerus fratrum tuorum sicut in actibus apostolorum 'augebatur' numerus 'credentium'.[2] Taliter enim diabolum superabis, et si quis ordini tuo et proposito causa rigidioris ordinis detraxerit, cum Iesu in Effrem habitans contempnes. Iam uero si requiratur a me quia sepe a multis queritur hoc cur ipsi de reditibus et decimis uiuant, quia his sacerdotes et leuitae sustentari per Moysen a Domino iubentur, simpliciter salua pace eorum qui forte hoc quod dicturus sum contradicturi sunt respondeo, quia qui altario seruiunt, cum altari participari debent, et qui sacerdotum et leuitarum onera in se ipsis quantum eis a predecessoribus concessum est refundunt, sacerdotis et leuitae mercede non debent omnino priuari.[3] Video enim aecclesias illorum uelint nolint a fidelibus frequentari, assidue eos missas cantare, frequenter euangelium predicare, ad sermonem faciendum in aecclesia cogi, peccata populi de carbone diuini altaris tangere,[4] et annuntiare 'populo scelera' sua,[5] lego etiam ut 'qui euangelium annuntiant de euangelio uiuant'[6] et 'dignus est operarius mercede sua',[7] et timeo eos inde iudicare, si accipiant quod ipsi merentur. Michi autem magis timeo, si inde eos iudicauero, ne ipse iudicer.[8] Potest enim in istis accipiendis esse simplex et mundus eorum

rule of an abbot are dwelling as it were with Jesus, flee lest you walk by the dark ways of the earth, and turn your face from the ways of the world and the dwellings of men, whose 'thoughts God knoweth that they are vain'.[1] Stay in Ephrem, seeking to grow and to increase the multiplicity of virtues and the number of your brothers, so that many shall be converted from the world by your good example and holy life, and the number of your brothers shall be increased, just as in the Acts of the Apostles the number of those who believed was increased.[2] In this way you shall overcome the devil, and if anyone slanders your order and way of life because of its rigour, you shall hold him of little worth, staying with Jesus in Ephrem. Now if it be asked of me, for it is often asked of many, why do they live on revenues and tithes, even though the priests and levites are ordered by God through Moses to maintain themselves on them, I reply simply, saving the peace of those who perhaps will contradict what I am about to say, that those who serve by the altar should share with the altar, and those who take on themselves the burdens of the priests and levites, as much as has been granted to them by their predecessors, ought not to be completely deprived of the wages of the priests and levites.[3] I see how their churches are frequented by the faithful, whether they desire it or not, how they constantly sing masses, frequently preach the Gospel, must give sermons in church, touch the sins of the people with the coal from the heavenly altar,[4] and show to the people their wicked doings.[5] I read also that 'those who proclaim the Gospel shall live from the Gospel',[6] and that 'the labourer is worthy of his hire',[7] and I am therefore loth to judge them if they take what they have earned. I myself fear to judge them all the more, lest I be judged.[8] Their disposition in accepting these things can be simple and pure, for it does not

30 (*Matteo XIII–8, nelle diverse interpretazioni*) (Rome [1953]), and Giovanni Miccoli, *Chiesa gregoriana* (Storici antichi e moderni, N.S. 7; Florence, 1966), pp. 5 and 56.

[1] Ps. 93: 11; 1 Cor. 3: 20.   [2] Acts 5: 14.

[3] On this and other passages dealing with tithes and parochial revenues, see Giles Constable, *Monastic Tithes from Their Origins to the Twelfth Century* (Cambridge Studies in Medieval Life and Thought, N.S. 10; Cambridge, 1964), pp. 154–5 and 178–9 (and 136–85 generally on the problem of performance of pastoral work and receipt of parochial revenues by monks and canons in the twelfth century).

[4] Isa. 6: 6–7. This passage was cited in a similar sense by Philip of Harvengt, *De institutione clericorum*, VI (77) (*PL*, cciii. 1102–3).   [5] Isa. 58: 1.

[6] 1 Cor. 9: 14.   [7] Luke 10: 7.   [8] Matt. 7: 1; Luke 6: 37.

affectus, qui non requirat superflua, sed expetat necessaria. Si autem dicatur non esse eorum illa accipere, dicatur etiam illa sanctiora eos non debere facere. Valde etiam indecorum est, ut tot monachorum agmina quae nos in Dei seruitio precesserunt, et nobiscum adhuc in uita manent pro una re causa scilicet ad litteram tuendae monasticae regulae, in qua ut ipse ait qui eam condidit 'non omnis iusticia' tradita est,[1] condempnare uelimus, presertim cum ipsi quod secundum regulam se obseruaturos esse[a] uouerunt, cum interrogantur super hoc bene se obseruare respondeant et confidant. Faueo bene intelligentibus, credo se obseruare regulam respondentibus, laudo secundum ordinem uniuscuiusque monasterii uiuentes, predico et apello dominos et patres, admiror et ueneror ipsam regulam etiam ad litteram omnino seruantes. Nulli enim derogare uolo, quem scio etiam si diuersa ab alterius intellectu sentiat, quod diuersa a fide christiana non teneat. Quod si inter se ipsi monachi de regula contendant, et dicat alter alteri quia laborare in agro debet, et talia indumenta qualia[b] in regula prescripta sunt habere, et illis uel illis epulis secundum regulam uti, intelligat qui hoc dicit et credat si quid a sapientibus aliter quam ipse intelligit uisum est, non frustra sed sapienter esse actum, ut uel multorum infirmitas reuelaretur, uel illorum qui se exemplo talium monachorum saluare cupiebant imbecillitas non terreretur. Ita ego eorum instituta facta esse intelligo, neutrum horum aestimans regulae suae preuaricatorem, et expeto uniuscuiusque orationes, quos scio in unitate fidei esse concordes. Non enim studeo aliquem de suo ordine reprehendere, sed ostendere cupio, quia licet diuerse uiuant, tamen ab uno principio ad unum finem Christum utrique suspirant. Habent enim et ipsi Dei serui qui inter homines uiuunt Christum inter homines ambulantem, habent etiam eundem propter incredulos ad tempus se diei festo subtrahentem,[2] et cum postea ascendit non manifeste sed quasi in occulto hoc fecit,[3] ut ignotesceret seruos Dei qui inter homines habitant aliquando propter homines saluos faciendos de alto mentis suae se oportere descendere, aliquando ne

15

---

[a] esse *add. supra*   [b] qualia *add. supra*

demand an excess, but looks for what is necessary. If you say
that it is not for them to take these things, you also say that they
should not carry out these holy duties. It is extremely improper
that we should wish to condemn so many companies of monks
who have gone before us in God's service, and are still with us
in this life, from just one consideration, that of abiding by the
letter of the monastic rule, in which, as he says who composed it,
'not all justice' is established,[1] particularly when they who have
vowed to observe the rule, when asked about this, answer that
they observe it well and believe in it. I applaud those who understand this; I believe those who answer they observe the rule;
I praise all those who live according to the order of each monastery;
I esteem them and call them lords and fathers; I admire and
revere those who observe the rule to the very letter; I wish to
blame no one even if I know he believes in a different interpretation, provided it is not at variance with the Christian faith.
15 And if these monks argue among themselves about the rule, and
one says to another that he should work in the fields and should
wear such clothing as is prescribed in the rule and should eat this
or that kind of food according to the rule, let him who says and
believes this understand that if anything seems different to wise
men from his understanding, it has been done wisely and not in
vain, either in order to accommodate the weakness of many or
in order that the weakness of those who wish to save their souls
through the example of such monks should not be alarmed. This
is the way in which I understand their usages grew up, and I judge
none of them to be transgressors of their rule, and I desire prayers
from each of those whom I know to be at one in the unity of
the faith, for I am not eager to blame anyone for his order, but
I desire to show that, though they live differently, they aspire
from one beginning to the one end which is Christ. For even
these servants of God who live among men find Christ walking
among men; they also have Him, who withdrew Himself for a
while on a feast day because of the unbelievers,[2] and later He went
up, 'not openly but as it were in secret',[3] so that the servants of
God who live among men might know that to bring salvation
to men they must sometimes come down from the height of their
contemplation, and at other times, lest the envy of the wicked

---

[1] Benedict, *Reg.*, LXXIII, tit.   [2] Gal. 2: 12.
[3] John 7: 10.

malorum liuor illis detrahat ad festum ubi 'reliquiae cogitationis'[1]
sunt id est peccatorum solutorum et remissorum recordatio diem
festum ubi Deus solus uidet cum saluatore suo occulte ascendere.
Pascant etiam nunc Iesum in seruis suis publicani et peccatores,
detrahant illi Pharisei, uerae scientiae ianuam claudentes, suscipiat Zacheus,[2] conuiuium faciat Leui,[3] ut sanus factus a medico
caelesti euangelium scribat. Monachus qui ita inter homines sicut
Iesus uiuit, non potest timere alium monachum qui sicut Phariseus
peccatricem a se repellit. Habebit et ipse qui regulam suam ad
litteram etiam bene seruat premium, si Iesum pro discipulis
suis 'per sata' huius uitae uel mundi[a] sabbato spicas uellentibus
id est ab hominibus uictum quaerentibus non reprehenderit.[4]
In sabbato enim discipuli Iesu spicas uellunt, quia feriati a
mundanis operibus uictum a mundanis hominibus quasi spicas
accipiunt. Sane monachorum regula ut legens aduerti sobrios
intellectores requirit, moderatosque lectores expetit. Nam multa
sunt quae sanctus ille ipsius regulae conditor non posuit, quia ea
indubitanter facienda nouerat, sicut est illud quod lectorem et
mensae ministros dicit antequam ad officium suum accedant debere
mixtum accipere[5] nec ullum excipit diem. Vnde quidam monachi
dicunt secundum regulam lectorem etiam in quadragesima debere
mixtum accipere, priusquam legat, quia hoc regula dicit, nec
ullum diem excipit, et ita cogunt ad comedendum bene ualentem
ieiunare. Alii uero econtra non accipiendum mixtum dicunt, quia
commune est et sollempne ieiunium. Bene isti dicunt. Sed audio
quosdam abstinentes monachos etiam die dominico secundum
beati Benedicti uitam quam in specu positus duxit argumentantes
debere uel posse ieiunare, quia omni die ieiunans etiam diem
dominicum non pretermittebat.[6] Vtrosque uideo, de utrisque quid

a uel mundi *add. supra*

slander them, they must go up in secret with their Saviour to the feast where 'the remainders of the thought'[1] are, that is the feast day of remembrance of the remission and forgiveness of sins, where God alone sees. May publicans and sinners now feed Jesus in His servants; may the Pharisees slander them, shutting the doors of true knowledge; may Zacchaeus receive Him;[2] may Levi make a feast,[3] so that made whole by the divine physician he may write the Gospel. A monk who thus lives like Jesus among men cannot fear another monk, who drives the sinful woman away from himself like the Pharisee. And he too who observes his rule to the letter shall have his reward if he does not blame Jesus on account of His disciples who plucked ears of corn on the sabbath in the fields of this life, or the world, that is who sought their sustenance from men.[4] For the disciples of Jesus pluck ears of corn on the sabbath because, taking a rest from worldly work, they take their sustenance like ears of corn from worldly men. Certainly the rule for monks requires men sober in understanding, as you can learn by reading it, and it demands readers of moderation. For there were many things which the holy author of that rule was not able to mention although without doubt he knew that they had to be done, as for example when he said that the lectors and servers at table should take a little bread and wine before starting their duties,[5] making no day an exception. For this reason some monks assert that according to the rule the lector should take bread and wine even in Lent before he starts his reading, since the rule says not one day should be excepted, and so they force people to eat even when they should clearly fast. Others on the contrary say that the bread and wine is not to be taken, since the fast is a solemn one and common to all. They speak well, but I hear certain abstinent monks arguing that they ought to fast and should be allowed to even on Sunday, since according to the life of St. Benedict, when he lived in a cave, he did not omit to fast every day, even on Sunday.[6] I see both points

---

[1] Ps. 75: 11.   [2] Luke 19: 1–10.   [3] Luke 5: 29.

[4] Mark 2: 23.   [5] Benedict, *Reg.*, XXXVIII, 10.

[6] Gregory, *Dial.*, II, I (ed. Moricca, pp. 77–8). St. Benedict had been living in a cave at Subiaco for three years when, according to Gregory, the Lord ordered a priest living some distance away to go and share his Easter meal with him. The priest found Benedict and said: 'Let us eat, for today is Easter.' Benedict had been away from other men for so long that he did not know it was Easter Sunday. The priest had to tell him again that it was Easter. 'It is not suitable

sentiam profero. Illi qui prandere bis etiam in quadragesima ualentes dicit, respondeo pro pace uniuersalis aecclesiae quae ieiunium
illud celebrat omnem hominem qui potest debere ieiunare, nec
esse contra regulam illam, quae licet quadragesimam uel sollempnia
ieiunia non exceperit,[a] pacem tamen aecclesiae seruare uoluit.
Non enim dignum est ut propter myxtum monachorum accipiant
occasionem ieiunii frangendi mensae potatorum, nec dignum est
ut[b] dicant edaces cum reprehensi pro soluto ieiunio fuerint, 'bene
hoc potest fieri, quia et monachi hoc faciunt'. Sic enim pro exiguo
cibo monachorum forsitan turbabitur religiosa institutio christianorum. Illi autem qui affirmat cotidie etiam dominico secundum
uitam beati Benedicti quam in specu positus seruauit posse
monachos ieiunare, respondeo, non ex me sed ex beati Gregorii
sententia qua dicit, 'quia longe ab hominibus positus', eo die quo
presbyter ad eum ex precepto Domini uenit quod 'paschalis esset
festiuitas ignorabat'. Quare fidenter dico, quia si ille sanctus
qui ignorabat dominicum diem et in ipso die ieiunabat laudandus
est, ille etiam presbyter predicandus est, qui ei dixit: 'Resurrectionis dominicae paschalis dies est, abstinere tibi minime conuenit,
quia et ad hoc missus sum, ut dona omnipotentis Dei pariter suma-
mus.' Ecce intuere, si post hanc uocem sacerdotis illius sanctus
ille ieiunauit, si abstinuit, si uocem Domini spreuit, et si potes
17 dominico die contende posse ieiunare. Quod uero in regula eorum
scriptum est et sine aliqua exceptione definitum, ut ab idibus
septembris usque ad nonam ieiunium extendant,[1] credo dominicum
diem ideo eum pretermisisse, quia sciebat illo die non esse ieiu-
nandum, nec inde aliquem dubitare, uel ob reuerentiam dominicae
resurrectionis, uel quia ita christiana consuetudo conualuit, ut eo
die ieiunare non liceat, ne scandalum in aecclesia generetur. Sunt
preterea quidam precipui dies, ut est natalis Domini, epyphania,
et similes dies, necnon et illius sancti in cuius honore cenobium
dedicatum est, ubi quidam timentes regulam offendere putant

---

[a] exciperit *corr.* exceperit   [b] dignum . . . ut *add. in marg.*

of view, and I shall give my opinion on both. To those who say that dining twice even in Lent is permissible, I reply for the peace of the universal church which celebrates this fast, that every man who can fast should, and it is not against the rule, even though he did not make an exception for Lent and solemn fasts, since he wished to keep the peace of the church. For it is not fitting that because of the bread and wine taken by monks, drinkers should have a pretext for breaking their fast at meal times, nor is it fitting that gluttons should say, when they are censured for breaking their fast: 'This may certainly be done, since even the monks do it.' In this way the religious institutions of Christians will perhaps be subverted because monks take a little food. To him who asserts that monks may fast every day, even on Sunday, according to the life of St. Benedict while he was in the cave, I reply not with my own opinion but with St. Gregory's, when he said that 'since he was far away from men' on the day the priest came to him by the Lord's command, he did not know it was Easter. In this case I say confidently that if the saint who did not know it was Sunday and who fasted on that day is to be praised, then the priest should also be honoured who said to him: 'This day is the Easter festival of the Lord's resurrection: it is not suitable for you to fast, because I was sent specially to share equally with you the gifts of almighty God.' See if after these words of the priest this holy man fasted and abstained, if he rejected God's word, and then, if you can, insist that one may fast on Sunday. With regard to what is written in their rule and laid down with no exceptions, the fast from September 13 lasts until the ninth hour,[1] and I believe he made no mention of Sunday because he knew that fasting was not required on that day, and that no one should doubt, either out of reverence for the Lord's resurrection or because Christian tradition confirms it, that fasting is not allowed on that day, lest scandal should arise in the church. Furthermore, there are certain special days, like Christmas, Epiphany, and the like, and also the feast days of the saints in whose honour the monastery is dedicated, when some people, fearing to offend against the rule, believe that the fast must be

for you to fast, because I was sent especially to share equally with you the gifts of almighty God.' They blessed God and ate, and when they had talked and eaten together a while the priest returned to his church.

[1] Benedict, *Reg.*, XLI, 6.

continuandum esse ieiunium. Volo autem omnes monachos et
canonicos siue clericos plus ieiunare et abstinere, quam plebeios
christianos, dignum est enim, sed uolo etiam supradictos uiros
communis gaudii christianorum in cibo et potu quantum uniuscuiusque regula patitur aliquando maxime in diebus sollemnibus
esse consortes, nec esse credo contra monachorum regulam quae
illos dies non excepit, si regula aecclesiastici gaudii ab eis etiam
qui seculi gaudia fugiunt obseruetur. Audio enim sepe cum talia
ieiunia in diebus ita sollemnibus custodiuntur multos inde mur-
murare, nec inde exemplum abstinentiae sumere, sed notam
absteritatis religiosis uiris impingere. Nec hoc dico, quasi reprehensor eorum qui perfectae student abstinentiae, sed uolo esse
18 consultum paci et laetitiae uniuersalis aecclesiae. Sane ne illud
quidem omittam, quod in utroque ordine tam monachorum quam
canonicorum sunt aliqui diuerso uitio laborantes, quorum alii
ita consuetudines suas tuentur, quasi in his 'iusticia constituta
sit',[1] nolentes aliquid pro tempore et loco et persona in aecclesia
mutari, alii uero ita fastidiosi sunt, ut nichil eis quod apud aecclesiam suam agatur placeat, sed semper noua sibi de alterius
monasterii consuetudine quae sociis imponant onera perquirant.
Vtrisque pro pace aecclesiae suae respondendum est. De illis qui
consuetudines suas ultra modum custodiunt, dicit Augustinus
in epistola de diuersis consuetudinibus aecclesiae Ianuario
notario directa:

Aliquis peregrinus in eo forte loco ubi perseuerantes in obseruatione
quadragesimae, nec quinta sabbati leuant, relaxantue ieiunium, non
inquit hodie ieiunabo. Queritur causa, quia non fit in patria mea. Quid
aliud iste, nisi consuetudinem suam consuetudini alterius preponere
conatur? Non enim michi de libro Dei hoc recitaturus est, aut uni-
uersae qua dilatatur aecclesiae plena uoce certabit, aut ostendet illum
contra fidem facere, se autem secundum fidem, moresque hinc opti-
mos aut illum uiolare aut se custodire conuincet. Violant sane quie-
tem et pacem de superflua questione rixando. Mallem tamen in rebus
huiusmodi, ut ille in huius et hic in illius patria, ab eo quod caeteri
faciunt non abhorreret.[2]

maintained. Now I desire all monks and canons or clerics to fast and abstain more than ordinary Christians, for it is fitting; but I also desire the men I have mentioned to share sometimes, especially on feast days, the common joy of Christians in eating and drinking, so far as their respective rules allow; and I do not believe that it is against the rule of the monks, which does not except those days, if the rule for rejoicing in the church is observed by those who avoid worldly rejoicing. For when such fasts are kept on feast days, I often hear many complaining about it and not taking from it an example of austerity, but attacking this mark of austerity in religious men. I do not say this in criticism of those who are zealous for perfect abstinence, but I wish to further the peace and joy of the universal church. Certainly I do not wish to fail to point out that in both orders, of monks and of canons, there are men labouring under different faults: some defend their customs as if 'justice were established' in them,[1] not wishing anything to be changed in the church to fit the time or the place or the persons; others are so fastidious that nothing done in their church pleases them, and they are for ever searching out new things for themselves from the usages of other monasteries, with which they then burden their brothers. Both kinds must be answered for the peace of the church. Of those who cling to their customs beyond moderation, Augustine says in his letter on the different customs of the church, written to the notary Januarius:

Suppose some one is travelling in a place where, in the continuous observance of Lent, people do not bathe or relax their fast on the fifth day of the week, and he says: 'I will not fast today'. He is asked why, and he says: 'Because it is not done in my country.' What is he doing but trying to make his own custom superior to another's custom? He will not quote me this from the book of God, nor assert it with the full voice of the universal church which is published everywhere, nor will he show that the other acts against the faith but he in accordance with it, nor will he prove that the other violates good morals, while he preserves them. To be sure, they both violate the peace and quiet of the church by quarrelling about a foolish question. I should prefer that each one would not repudiate the custom of the other's country, but each do what the others do.[2]

[1] Benedict, *Reg.*, LXXIII, tit.
[2] Augustine, *Ep.* 54, IV, 5 (*CSEL*, xxxiv. 163–4; tr. Sister Wilfrid Parsons [Fathers of the Church, ix], p. 256).

Haec Augustinus de his qui ultra modum consuetudines suas custodire uolunt. De his autem qui cito mutant consuetudines, dicit in eadem epistola:

Faciat quisque, quod in ea aecclesia ad quam uenit inuenit. Non enim quicquam eorum contra fidem est, aut mores fiunt hinc uel inde meliores. His enim causis, id est aut propter mores, uel emendari oportet quod perperam fiebat, uel institui quod non fiebat. Ipsa quippe mutatio consuetudinis, etiam quae utilitate adiuuat, tamen nouitate perturbat. Quapropter quae utilis non est, perturbatione infructuosa consequenter noxia est.[1]

Haec etiam dicit de his qui nouas et alienas consuetudines sequuntur. Caeterum lectoris prudentia uideat quia et in tenendis ultra modum suis consuetudinibus, et in sequendis alienis, potest scisma et perturbatio generari. Vnde oportet unamquamque aecclesiam ita uetera custodire ut pro loco et tempore laxentur, et ita noua condere, ut ex nouitate antiqua patrum auctoritas non uioletur. Vellem autem inter monachos uniuscuiusque prouintiae similiter et canonicos esse ut inuicem se sequerentur, ut qui in una prouintia degunt, uno modo ieiunarent, una consuetudine silentia tenerent, de his autem loquor, qui in ciuitatibus et castellis habitant. Forsitan enim utrumque ita melius ac libentius teneretur, quia si quis ea quae ab omnibus tenerentur infringeret, se magis errasse fateretur, et forte citius corrigeretur. Sicut enim ieiunium quod a patribus obseruatum est, et ab omnibus ritu communi tenetur, melius ac libentius etiam inter laicos obseruatur, quam illud quod nouiter inuentum est nec ab omnibus tenetur, faciliusque redarguitur qui infringit, ita credo fieret inter monachos et canonicos, si omnes obseruantiam unam sequerentur, essetque laudabilis supra omne ieiunium concordia, ubi omnes unam unius ordinis tenerent uiuendi mensuram. Sed quia uidemus etiam in uno loco alios solito more uelle prandere, alios contra morem antiquum uelle ieiunare, oritur hinc sane rixa intolerabilis, quia alius ex auctoritate se credit facere quod facit, alius zelo iusticiae se credit accendi. Vnde aliquando inter tales superbia

This is what Augustine says about those who wish to cling to their customs beyond moderation. Of those who quickly change their customs he says in the same letter:

> Let each one, then, do what he finds in that church which he attends. For none of these usages is contrary to the faith, nor do morals become better by one or other of them. For these reasons, that is, because of [faith or] morals, what is wrongly done should be corrected, and what is not done should be begun. But the mere change of custom, though it may be helpful, may also be disturbing because of novelty. Therefore what is not helpful is a source of fruitless and, consequently, harmful disturbance.[1]

This then is what he says of those who follow new and foreign customs. Let the prudence of the reader see the rest, that in retaining one's own customs too rigorously, and in following foreign ones, schisms and disturbances can be generated. For this reason every church should so retain the old ways, relaxed in accordance with the time and the place, and so introduce new ones, that the ancient authority of the fathers is not violated by 19 novelties. I would wish that the monks of the same province, and the canons similarly, should follow each other mutually, so that those who live in one province should fast in the same way and follow the same rule of silence. I am speaking of those who live in cities and towns. Perhaps then both rules would be better maintained and more willingly, since were anyone to infringe those rules which are observed by everyone he would confess his fault all the more and perhaps more quickly correct it. In the same way, a fast which was observed by the fathers and is maintained by all in a common rite is better and more willingly observed even among the laity than one which has been recently invented and is not kept by all. The man who breaks it can be more easily confuted; so it would also be, I believe, among monks and canons if they all followed one observance, and there would exist a harmony more praiseworthy than all fasting, where all held a single measure of life of one order. But because we find in one place some wishing to dine as is customary and some wishing to fast against the established custom, an intolerable wrangling develops, since one thinks that he does what he does with authority and the other thinks that he burns with the zeal of righteousness. And so from

---

[1] Augustine, *Ep.* 54, v, 6 (*CSEL*, xxxiv. 165–6; tr. Parsons, p. 257).

et inuidia nascitur, ut qui ieiunare uolunt contra non ieiunantes superbiant, et qui non ieiunant, ieiunantibus inuideant. Proinde accedit grauior morbus, ut illi qui propter ieiunium superbiunt non contenti secum habitantes despicere, etiam alienos a suo proposito et aecclesia quia similiter sicut ipsi uolunt non ieiunant despicere non reformidant. Audiui enim quendam et nisi puderet dicere plures uano tumore turgidos, detrahentes ordini alterius aecclesiae, et dicentes: 'Qualis ordo est, ubi sic prandetur, tam parum ieiunatur, tam parum siletur, tot fercula sepe sumuntur?' Ad laudem aecclesiae suae et ordinis hoc se putant dicere, sed uide quid inde incurrant. Primum ad cumulum superbiae et ut ita dicam fastigium inde ducuntur, et tam alta fit ipsa superbia ut uideri non possit, et dum non aduertitur esse superbia, creditur humilitas, deinde, dum despicitur proximus, contempnitur Christus. Redeat ergo quisquis talis est ad se, non efferat se super se, ne despiciendo unum de his pusillis qui in Iesum credunt, de alto superbiae cadat, et dignus Christi uoce iudicetur, cui 'mola asinaria de collo suspendatur, et in mare' proiciatur.[1] Discat ab apostolo 'et habundare et penuriam pati',[2] inuitet etiam fratrem suum si aecclesia eius patitur, ad id quod idem ait, 'bonum est non manducare carnem et non bibere uinum',[3] hoc est, perfecte abstinere a cibis corporalibus, quantum uniuscuiusque capacitas sinit,[a] sciens etiam 'nichil abiciendum' ab his qui hoc adhuc aggredi nolunt, 'quod cum gratiarum actione percipitur'.[4] Noverit etiam, non cibum, sed cibi appetitum in culpa esse.[5] Nam et Esau uilis lenticulae desiderio exardescens, qui sepe uenationes fastidiebat eo desiderio primogenita perdidit,[6] et e contrario Dauid desideria refrenans, non uini sed aquae pocula captans, ipsam Domino sacrificando, se ipsum iustificauit.[7] Male ergo facit, qui de uilibus cibis uentrem ingurgitat, bene facit, qui etiam de uilibus modum tenet. Bene etiam facit, qui bona quae in macello ueniunt[8] cum mensura et gratiarum actione sumit, deterior

---

[a] sinit *add. supra*

time to time pride and envy arise among such men, with those
wishing to fast showing arrogance to those who do not, and those
who do not showing envy of those who do. In this way too a worse
disease flares up, so that those who are proud of their fasting, not
content with despising those they live with, do not fear to despise
even strangers to their usages and church, since they do not fast
in the way they want them to. Indeed I have heard someone, and
(except that it is shameful to say so) several people swollen with
empty bombast, slandering the customs of another church and
saying: 'What kind of rule is that, where there is so much eating
and so little fasting, so little silence and so many courses are
always being eaten?' They think they speak in praise of their own
church and order, but see what it leads them to. First they are
led to the mountain and, as I might say, to the very peak of pride,
and this pride soars so high that it cannot be seen, and since it is
not perceived as pride it is believed to be humility; then Christ
is despised, in that their neighbour is despised. Let every one of
such men return to himself and not raise himself above his own
level, lest by despising one of those little ones who believe in
Jesus he fall from the height of his pride, worthy to be judged, in
Christ's words, to have a millstone hung about his neck and be
cast into the sea.[1] May he learn from the apostle 'both to abound
and to suffer need';[2] if his church allows it, let him also invite his
brother to do what the same man said 'is good, not to eat flesh
and not to drink wine',[3] that is to abstain perfectly from bodily
food to the degree that each one's capacity allows, knowing that
from those who do not yet wish to undertake it 'nothing is to be
rejected that is received with thanksgiving'.[4] Let him also know
that food is not sinful but the appetite for food.[5] For Esau,
obsessed with a hunger for paltry lentils, who often scorned the
meat from hunting, lost his birthright through that hunger.[6]
But on the other hand David, restraining his appetite and taking
a cup of water rather than wine, sacrificed it to God and justified
himself.[7] He does ill, therefore, who fills his belly with mean food.
He does well who takes it in moderation. He also does well who
takes those good things which are sold in the meat-market[8]

[1] Matt. 18: 6; Mark 9:41.   [2] Phil. 4: 12.
[3] Rom. 14: 21.   [4] 1 Tim. 4: 4.
[5] Cf. Gregory, *Moralia*, xxx, 60 (*PL*, lxxvi. 557B).
[6] Gen. 25: 34.   [7] 2 Kgs. 23: 16; 1 Para. 11: 18.
[8] 1 Cor. 10: 25.

omnibus est, qui etiam quaecunque sibi deferuntur aut fastidit, aut preciose uel laute confici gestit. Ascendat igitur qui potest et sequatur abstinentiores, condescendat abstinens et caritatem minus ualido prebeat, ut infirmum fratrem expectans cum eo in peruentione cursus gaudeat, ut uterque in uia Dei obicem non sentiens brauium aeternae remunerationis accipiat.[1] Discant

20 pusillanimes confortari, discant fortes humiliari. Ad postremum uero ne illud omittam, quod ipsi monachi qui in urbibus et uicis morantur, secularia sepius tractare uidentur, forensia iudicia decernunt, seruos habent et ancillas capitales, iudicant, regunt, tuentur, filios seruorum seruos futuros nutriunt,[a] terras hospitales habent, ad censum dant, redditus inde sperant, et exigunt, causas singulorum ueluti iudices seculares audiunt, leges suis terris et hominibus imponunt, quae omnia secularia et minus religiosa esse uidentur. De talibus tamen dicam quod sentio. Non hoc credo ab eis inuentum esse propter cupiditatem, sed propter seruorum et hospitum utilitatem. Nam uidemus multos feroces dominos fugientes sub dominio aecclesiarum confugere, in quibus tuendis et defensandis non cupiditas ulla, sed misericordia est maxima.[2] Quodammodo enim, cum fugitiuos suscipiunt, urbes fugitiuorum in possessione sanctorum sicut ille antiquus populus constituerunt. Si autem dicat aliquis non ideo debere monachos de secularibus se intromittere, illum admoneo qui hoc dicit ut sobrius reprehensor sit, nec ante tempus quicquam iudicet,[3] quia lego et Iacob post amplexus desideratae Rachelis ad Liae fertilis concubitum redisse,[4] id est illos qui gustauerunt dulcedinem contemplatiuae uitae, ad agenda opera actiuae uitae, non propter se, sed propter alios redisse. Aequalem enim uideo esse misericordiam et in defensandis pro posse ab iniquis pauperibus, et in

---

[a] nutriunt, seruos futuros *corr.* seruos futuros nutriunt

in moderation and with thanksgiving. Worst of all is he who either despises whatever is brought to him or desires it to be prepared richly and elegantly. Let him who can arise and follow the more abstinent; let him in his self-denial stoop to offer charity to the less worthy, so that in looking out for his weak brother he may rejoice with him in running the race, so that both, finding no obstacles on the path to God, may receive the prize of eternal reward.[1] Let the fainthearted take comfort. Let the strong learn humility. And finally, I should not omit mention of those monks who live in cities and villages and are seen often to deal with secular matters, making decisions on public lawsuits, owning serfs and bondwomen, judging, ruling, protecting, bringing up the sons of their serfs as future serfs, owning lands held by tenants, renting out lands, hoping for and exacting revenues therefrom, judging cases of individuals like secular judges, imposing laws on their lands and men, all of which seems secular and hardly religious. Of such men I shall say what I think: I do not believe that they have become involved in all this through cupidity, but for the sake of their serfs and tenants, for we see many men fleeing from cruel masters and taking refuge under the lordship of churches, and in assuming their protection and defence there is no cupidity at all but the greatest charity.[2] In a way, when they take in fugitives they found cities of refuge in the possession of the saints, like the people of antiquity. If anyone should say that monks ought not to interfere in secular matters like this, I admonish him to be more sober in his judgements, and not to censure anything prematurely,[3] for I read that Jacob, after embracing Rachel whom he desired, returned to cohabitation with the fertile Leah.[4] This means that those who have enjoyed the sweetness of the contemplative life have returned to an active life of works, not on account of themselves but of others. I consider defending the poor from the wicked to the best of one's

---

[1] 1 Cor. 9: 24.

[2] The fugitives in question here and below are not fugitive monks from other monasteries, as suggested by Jean Leclercq, 'Documents sur les "fugitifs"', *Analecta monastica*, vii (Studia Anselmiana, 54; Rome, 1965), p. 108, but laymen fleeing to monastic estates from the harsh treatment of other landlords. Peter the Venerable in his letter 28 to St. Bernard also made the point that monks treated the workers on their estates much better than lay landlords: *The Letters of Peter the Venerable*, ed. Giles Constable (Harvard Historical Studies, 78; Cambridge, Mass., 1967) i. 86–7. Cf. introd., pp. xxi–xxii.

[3] 1 Cor. 4: 5.

[4] Gen. 29: 16–29.

nutriendis uel suscipiendis hominibus. Quod si quis reprehendat
eos quae pauperum sunt uel hospitum suorum suscipere, legat
Dominum dixisse, 'reddite Cesari quae Cesaris sunt, et Deo
quae Dei sunt',[1] nec miretur amplius si monachis reddant quae
Cesaris sunt, quos fugitiui ipsi Cesares propter tutamen sui et
uxorum et filiorum et possessionum constituerunt. Non enim
semper propter se monachi hoc agunt, sed propter ipsos, qui
licet seculares sint, tamen a sanctis uiris auxilium protectionis
21 exposcunt. Sed dicat adhuc aliquis: Si ergo bonum est ut eos
sustentent, ut protegant, ut nutriant, quid est quod aliquando
ipsos in carcerem mittunt, uerberant, leges sumunt, sua auferunt?
Ad hoc respondeo in his modum debere seruari, ut in carcerem
missi non deficiant, ut uerberati a talibus non moriantur, ut
leges dantes pauperes ultra modum non efficiantur, nec propter
uindictam ista exerceantur, sed propter correctionem caeterorum
seruorum et hospitum suorum, ut haec uidentes caeteri timorem
habeant, et mala facere formident. Melius est enim et in ordinibus
et in secularibus ut unus uapulet et saluetur cum multis, quam ut
effrenata humanitas quae uix etiam cum ei mala et plagae pro
criminibus inferuntur se cohibere potest, accepta per misericordiam peccandi licentia dispereat. In talibus etiam exercendis
ipsi monachi modum debent aptum tenere, ne ipsi in his agendis
mensuram excedant, ut appareat eos ad haec non ex uoluntate
propria ferri, sed pauperum necessitati et utilitati consulere. Ad
haec etiam agenda non debet infirma aetas laxari, nec nouiter
conuersi ad haec cito remitti, quia sepe alta cedrus ista agens a
statu concutitur, quanto magis nouella planta si uento secularitatis
coeperit tangi, non citius eradicabitur? Fortassis ista dicens aliquos
sanctioris propositi uiros offendo, sed hoc paci aecclesiae pro
posse consulens dico, credens et sperans, quod omnia quae in
aecclesiis Christi in una fide manentibus obseruantur summo
pontifici placeant, nec oblationem uniuscuiusque quamlibet
parua sit pius sacerdos respuat, quae de corde contrito et spiritu
humiliato offeratur. Haec de monachis qui in ciuitatibus et castellis
et similibus locis manent diximus, alterius intellectum qui melius

ability and feeding and looking after men equally merciful. And if anyone blames them for taking what belongs to the poor or to their tenants, let him read the words of the Lord: 'Render therefore to Caesar the things that are Caesar's; and to God the things that are God's',[1] and let him no longer be surprised if they render to the monks what is Caesar's, which Caesars the fugitives themselves established for the protection of themselves and their wives and children and property. The monks do not always do this on their own account but for those who, though of the world, nevertheless beg for the help and the protection of holy men. But someone will now say: If it is good that they sustain, protect, and feed them, why do they sometimes put men in prison, beat them, enforce the laws, and take away their goods? To this I reply that a mean must be maintained in these matters, so that prisoners are not in want, that those beaten by such men do not die, that laws affecting the poor should not become excessive and should not be enforced from vengefulness but for the correction of their other serfs and tenants, so that on seeing this the others will be afraid and will avoid wrong-doing. For it is better, both in religious orders and in the world, that one man should be flogged and saved with the many, than that humanity should perish unrestrained, which can barely check itself even when evils and plagues are visited on it on account of its crimes, having been allowed to sin through lenience. When carrying out such duties the monks must use restraint lest they exceed due moderation, and it must be clear that they do these things not arbitrarily but out of consideration for the needs and welfare of the poor. For this it is necessary that such duties should not be entrusted to those of tender years nor too quickly to newcomers to the monastic life, since if the high cedar acting in this way is often blown from its place, how much more quickly is the new plant uprooted when the winds of the world begin to blow on it? Perhaps in saying this I offend some men of a more holy way of life, but I say it keeping the peace of the church in mind to the best of my ability, believing and trusting that everything observed in Christ's churches by those abiding in one faith pleases the highest pontiff and that the pious priest will not reject the sacrifice of any man, no matter how small, if it is offered with a contrite heart and a humble spirit. We have said these things of monks living in cities and towns and

[1] Matt. 22: 21; Mark 12: 17; Luke 20: 25

senserit amplectentes, et lectorem deprecantes, ut si aliquid prauum diximus non maliuolentiae deputet, sed si quid boni scriptum est diligat, si uero aliquid mali fidenter corrigat, et nobis qui melius dicere nescimus indulgeat.

III. *De monachis qui longe se ab hominibus faciunt, ut Cistercienses et si qui sunt similes.*

22 Iam uero ad illos stilus recurrat, qui monachi nomen a turbis omnino seggregati insigniunt, de quorum uita et instituto aliquid sinistrum suspicari non licet, nec inde loquentem ne in laude ipsorum quantamcumque dixerit peccet, timere oportet. Sunt enim in locis suis ita uiuentes, ut in carne manentes quia carnalia deserunt et transcendunt, supra carnem esse iure dicantur. Miratur enim quisquis eos uidet humanae infirmitatis tantam immutationem, nec iam esse de terra, sed esse in terra asseruntur. Intueamur tamen, si alicubi in antiquis tale aliquid inueniamus. Scriptum est in libro regum tercio, quod Abdias minister regis Achab tempore persequutionis et famis 'centum prophetas in speluncis per quinquagenos diuisos aluit pane et aqua'.[1] Aiunt etiam Hebraei et beatus Ieronimus assentit,[2] quod ipse sit Abdias, qui inter duodecim minores annumeratur, et propterea datum ei esse spiritum Domini, quod prophetas spiritum Dei habentes pauerit. Interpretatur uero Abdias seruus Domini.[3] Quia uero habemus seruum Domini prophetas pascentem, et habemus tempus famis et persequutionis, et centum prophetas pro perfectione, quia talis numerus in scripturis diuinis pro perfectione accipitur, et quinquagenos pro remissione, quia et in lege annus quinquagesimus remissionis appellabatur, eo quod in eo a seruitute remittebantur, et possessiones recipiebant, et in iubilatione

23 relaxabantur, intueamur quantum faueat antiqua hystoria nostro tempori, in quo si non idem forte, tamen simile quid agitur. Nam et in nostro tempore tales Dei seruos illi qui terrena negotia habent in abditis et remotis terrarum suarum locis mittunt, ut precum suarum effusione illorum peccata redimant, et ut[a] ipsi

a ut et *corr.* et ut

such places, embracing the opinion of anyone else who sees more clearly and begging the reader that if we have said anything wicked, he will not attribute it to malice; but if anything good has been written, he will love it; and if indeed anything evil, he will confidently correct it and be indulgent towards us since we did not know how to speak better.

III. *Monks who remove themselves far from men, such as the Cistercians and the like.*

Now let my pen return to those who are known by the name of monk and who live completely cut off from the multitudes, of whose life and regime no one may suspect anything untoward, nor need anyone fear lest he sin no matter how much he may say in their praise. They so live in their houses that, remaining in the flesh, since they forsake and transcend the fleshly, they are justly said to be above the flesh. Let anyone who sees them wonder at such a change in human infirmity, for though they are on the earth they are said to be not of it. Let us see whether we can find anything like it anywhere in antiquity. It is written in the third book of Kings that Abdias, the servant of King Achab, at a time of persecution and famine, concealed 'a hundred prophets in caves by fifty and fifty and fed them with bread and water'.[1] And the Hebrews say, and St. Jerome agrees, that this is the same Abdias who is numbered among the twelve minor prophets and who was given the spirit of God because he had fed the prophets who had the spirit of God.[2] Abdias means servant of the Lord.[3] For truly we have a servant of the Lord feeding the prophets, and we have a time of famine and persecution, and a hundred prophets for perfection, since this number in Holy Scripture is interpreted as perfection, and fifty means remission, since in the law the fiftieth year was called the year of remission, and since they were released from servitude then and received their possessions and took their liberty rejoicing. We see how much ancient history approves what is done today, what occurs is similar even if perhaps not identical. For in our day too those men who have worldly concerns send into hidden and remote parts of their lands such servants of God who by pouring out their prayers may redeem the price of those [other] men's sins, so that they also

---

[1] 3 Kgs. 18: 3–4.   [2] Jerome, *In Abdiam*, ad 5. 1 (*PL*, xxv. 1099A).
[3] Jerome, *Nom. heb.* (*CC*, lxxii. 124).

spiritum Dei sicut et illi accipiant. Fit uero et hoc tempore persequutionis, quando regina impiissima Iezabel id est superbia et luxus seculi seruos Dei uehementer infestos habet, et quoscunque potest seducendo necat.[1] Contingit etiam haec tempore famis, quando quaeritur qui iusticiam teneat, qui ueritatem seruet, qui aliena non rapiat, qui uerbum Dei puro corde predicet, et uix inuenitur, ut impleatur etiam in nobis illud Ysaiae: 'Immittam famem in terra', et caetera.[2] Et illud: 'Preciosior erit uir auro, et homo similiter obrizo.'[3] Additur etiam quod centum pauerit, ut 'perfecta caritas foras mittens seruilem timorem',[4] accipiat 'timorem castum permanentem in seculum seculi',[5] et ita Abdias qui interpretatur seruus Domini fiat, et sicut ille prophetico dono participauit, sic iste seruorum nutritor et institutor eorum uitam diligens et imitari cupiens, ad hoc quandoque perducatur, ut quod illi agunt et ipse agat, et sic ipsorum spiritu inflammatus inardescat. Videmus enim sepe tales homines, qui cum essent seculares, et rerum affluentia et uoluptatum copia habundarent nec ab hominibus in eis esse aliqua uirtus animi deprehenderetur, nisi hoc solum quod seruos Dei instituebant et nutriebant, ad hoc uenisse, ut pauperes effecti pauperem Christum sequerentur,[6] et tollentes crucem suam artam et arduam uiam[7] monachorum aggrederentur, et redderent homines humana tantum sapientes admiratos et stupidos in subitatione insperatae salutis, ita ut diceretur de eis: 'Haec est immutatio dexterae excelsi',[8] nouit enim Dominus qui sunt eius. Nam et ipse Abdias persequutor esse sancti Heliae credebatur eo quod minister regis persequutoris esset, et tamen quod amator esset etiam minorum seruorum Dei quam Helias prorsus latebat. Diuisi etiam ipsi sunt ab eo per quinquagenos in speluncis, quia caritatem Dei et proximi tales serui Dei in corde perfecte retinentes quod significatur per speluncas remissionem plenariam postmodum cum seruis Dei ipsi Deo militantes assequuntur, quod per quinquaginta indicatur. Quomodo autem

will receive the spirit of God like them. This also happens in a time of persecution, when the most impious queen Jezebel, that is pride and love of the world, has the servants of God violently molested and destroys whomever she can by her seduction.[1] These things also happen in a time of famine, when someone is sought out to uphold justice, to serve truth, who will not steal the property of others and who will preach God's word with a pure heart—and they are scarcely to be found, so that the words of Isaiah are fulfilled in us: 'I will send in upon you famine', and so on;[2] and these: 'A man shall be more precious than gold: yea and a man than the finest of gold.'[3] It is added that he fed a hundred, so that 'perfect charity casting out slavish fear'[4] should receive a 'chaste fear enduring for ever and ever';[5] and as it happened with Abdias, which means servant of the Lord, and just as he shared in that gift of prophesy, so this feeder and lodger of servants, loving and desiring to imitate their life, may be led sometimes to do what they do and burn afire with their spirit. We often see that such men who, though they were of the world and abounded in material riches and a host of pleasures, with no one able to perceive in them any spiritual virtue, except that they fed and housed God's servants, have come to this, so that made poor, they followed the poor Christ[6] and bearing His cross entered into the strait and arduous life of monks;[7] and they have made worldly-wise men amazed and astonished by the suddenness of their unhoped-for salvation, so that it was said of them: 'This is the change of the right hand of the most High',[8] for God knows who are His own. Even Abdias was believed to be a persecutor of St. Elias, since he was a servant of a persecuting king, but the fact that he was also a lover of God's lesser servants than Elias was not known. They also were divided by him into fifties in caves, because such servants of God keeping the love of God and their neighbour perfectly in their hearts, which are signified by the caves, afterwards themselves fighting for God with God's servants attained complete remission, which is signified by fifty. How did they

---

[1] Cf. Rev. 2: 20. [2] Ezech. 5: 17. [3] Isa. 13: 12.
[4] 1 John 4: 18. [5] Ps. 18: 10.
[6] This theme occurs frequently in twelfth-century monastic literature: see Matthäus Bernards, 'Nudus nudum Christum sequi', *Wissenschaft und Weisheit*, xiv (1951), 148–51, to whose examples can be added many others, emphasizing the imitation of both the nudity and the poverty of Christ.
[7] Cf. Matt. 7: 14; Luke 13: 24. [8] Ps. 76: 11.

assequuntur? Numquid non assecuntur plenam remissionem, qui
liberati a seculari tumultu soli Deo militant,[1] et si quid molle, si
quid dissolutum[2] in domibus regum uel principum huius seculi[a]
in usu habuerunt, agnum paschalem Christum succinctis renibus[3]
id est restrictis huius corruptionis illecebris comedentes, 'ab
ubertate domus Dei inebriantur'?[4] Sic enim diuiduntur per
quinquagenos, quia caritatem erga Deum habentes prius ab eo
remissionem accipiunt, et caritatis officia erga fratres tenentes si
quid alicui tulerant, si quid mali fecerant, si quid dixerant, uiso
tanto professionis eorum decore, libentissime eis preterita peccata
24 quae in se fuerant commissa relaxant. Diximus de eo et eius
similibus qui prophetas abscondit, quantum profecerit, quid
assequutus sit, quid de eis dicturi sumus qui absconsi sunt?
Intueamur ergo eorum uitam, qualis eo tempore fuerit, cum et
caritas principis eis necessaria uitae subministrabat, et separatio
a mundana conuersatione tumultum omnem refrenabat. De
abstinentia uero eorum si loqui uoluero superfluus iudicabor, cum
ipsi pane et aqua quod est commune et forte ieiunium uterentur,
ut abstinenter uiuentes in laudem Dei extenuarentur, nec cibis
corpulentioribus grauati pondere carnis impedirentur, sed
graciles facti, corpore tenues, mente subtiles, spiritu qui in libro
sapientiae subtilis et mobilis dicitur[5] leues facti ipsi replerentur.
Sed et ipsi prophetae qui coram Heliseo propheta manebant, in
quorum olla puer inscius mortiferum quid immisit[6] uide quam
sobrie uixerint, qui esuriem corporis herbis aggrestibus depelle-
bant. Non hoc dico quasi credam in his sumendis uel non sumendis
iusticiam esse statutam,[7] cum haec agentem premia non sequantur,
nisi ista pax et iusticia et misericordia precesserint, sed quia post
25 illa et haec agentem multipliciora Dei dona comitentur. Inspice
ergo homines illos et nostri etiam temporis monachos similiter
uiuentes, quam concors spiritus simul coadunauerit,[8] ut unum
spiritum habentes simul uiuerent, unum sentirent, in nullo
discrepare in alterutrum, uolentes similiter comederent, uno cultu
et modo induerentur, ut animi concordia per exteriorem habitus

---

[a] seculi *add. supra*

attain it? Will not they who fight alone for God freed from secular business[1] attain a full remission, and if in the houses of kings or princes of this world they made use of anything loose or anything slack,[2] eating the paschal lamb Christ with loins girded,[3] that is restrained from the allurements of this corruption, shall they not 'be inebriated with the plenty of God's house'?[4] Thus they were divided into fifties, for having the love of God they first accepted remission from Him and fulfilling the duties of charity towards their brothers, if they had taken anything from anyone, if they had done anything evil, if they had said anything, by virtue of the great honour of their profession, whatever sins they had previously committed were most freely forgiven. We have spoken of him and those like him who hid the prophets, of how much he gained and what he attained; what shall we say of those who were hidden? Let us examine the life they led at that time, when both the charity of a prince supplied the necessities of life to them and separation from the world suppressed all disturbance. If I wish to speak of their abstinence, I should be judged to speak superfluously, since they used bread and water, which form the common and strict fast, so that those living abstinently became thin in praising God and, not weighed down by more corporeal food, were not hindered by weight of flesh, but, made lean, slender in body, subtle in mind, and light, were filled themselves with that spirit which in the book of Wisdom is called subtle and active.[5] But even those prophets who stayed with Eliseus the prophet, into whose pot an ignorant boy put something deadly,[6] see how soberly they lived who picked the herbs of the field for their bodily hunger. I do not say this believing that justice is fulfilled[7] in eating or not eating certain things, since rewards do not follow such actions unless peace and justice and mercy have gone before, but after them and such actions the manifold gifts of God follow. Look at those men and at the monks even of our own day who live similarly, how harmony of mind has been added to spirit,[8] and having one spirit they live together, feel as one, wishing to differ in nothing one from another, eat similarly, adopting one kind of worship and way of life, so that concord of soul should be

---

[1] Cf. 2 Tim. 2: 4.
[2] Prov. 18: 9.
[3] Cf. Ephes. 6: 14; 1 Pet. 1: 13.
[4] Ps. 35: 9.
[5] Wisd. 7: 23-4.
[6] 4 Kgs. 4: 40.
[7] Benedict, *Reg.*, LXXIII, tit.
[8] Cf. Phil. 1: 27; Eph. 4: 3.

consonantiam panderetur. Neque enim credo eosdem antiquos
prophetas communi hominum habitu usos fuisse, ubi prout
cuilibet quisque uestem suam immutat, sed fuisse in eis existimo
quod in monachis diuersi ordinis inspicitur, qui multociens
solummodo uisi nec interrogati ex habitus indicio recognoscuntur
unde sint, uel cuius professionis uel monasterii. Inde est illud
quod inuenio regem Israel signa uiri Dei Heliae seruos suos
interrogasse, et quia 'uir pilosus et zona pellicia accinctus renibus'[1]
pronuntiatus est, Helias Thesbites esse a rege proclamatus est.
Vnde credo et inter illos qui in urbibus morabantur et inter eos
qui heremum incolebant sicut Helias qui pilosus erat aliquam
etiam in habitu habuisse distantiam, ut in his qui iuxta homines
morabantur quaedam morigera et moderatior uestis esset, hi
uero qui heremum incolebant in testimonium rigidioris instituti
hispidas et duras uestes haberent. Neque enim credo Ysaiam et
Heliam uno habitu prophetasse, cum ille esset nobilis et urbanus,
et ut legitur regis Ezechiae socer,[2] hic uero populorum cateruas
frequenter fugiens rigidius uixerit. Sed de habitu siue istorum
siue aliorum ut in prefatione promisimus, alias Deo donante
26 dicemus. Sed qui de abstinentia prophetarum et monachorum uel
de habitu loquimur, quid de caritate, de misericordia, de elemo-
sina, et hospitalitate, et caeteris uirtutibus dicemus? Superfluum
credo inde multum loqui, nisi ut inde alii accendantur, cum ad
tales aduentantes magis in seruis Dei ista experiri contigerit,
quam nos aliquid uerum loqui. Susceptus est a prophetantibus
benigne Saul, etiam cum sanctum Dauid persequeretur, et facto
in se spiritu Dei prophetauit,[3] et inuitus pronuntiauit, quod
apostolus dicit, quia uere 'Deus in uobis est'.[4] Suscipiuntur etiam
a monachis similiter ut prophetae uiuentibus, qui eis sua auferre
moliuntur, ita ut audierimus a quibusdam, quod illi qui rapere
uenerant, uel rapaces extiterant, uiso humilitatis eorum proposito,
uel monachi facti remanserint, uel accusantes se ipsos quod talia
assequi dona digni non fuerint, pacifici ad propria recesserint.
Operantur etiam ipsi quaecunque sibi a prelatis iniunguntur cum
tanta beniuolentia, ut iure de eis dici possit, quod nullum eos

expressed by an outer consonance of appearance. Not that I believe the ancient prophets used a habit common to all, but each one changed his clothing as it pleased him, but I assume that there was in them what is seen in the monks of various orders, many of whom can be recognized by sight purely from the design of their clothing without being asked where they are from or of what order or monastery. I find this when I read that the king of Israel asked his servants what was the sign of the man of God Elias, and hearing that he was 'a hairy man with a girdle of leather about his loins',[1] the king declared that he was Elias the Thesbite. And so I believe that between those who lived in cities and those who lived in the desert, like Elias, who was hairy, there was a certain diversity of clothing: those men who lived near other men wore the customary and average dress and those who lived in the desert wore rough and coarse clothes, attesting to a more rigorous way of life. And I do not think that Isaiah and Elias prophesied in the same clothing, for one was noble and a city-dweller and, as is written, father-in-law of King Ezechias,[2] while the other, often fleeing from crowds of people, lived a harder life. But as we promised in our preface, we shall speak elsewhere, 6 God willing, of the various kinds of habit. But what shall we, who are discussing the abstinence of the prophets and monks and their habit, say of their charity, mercy, almsgiving, hospitality, and other virtues? I should think it superfluous to say much of these things, except in order thereby to arouse others, since more can be learned of such matters from the servants of God than from the truth of anything I can say. Saul was kindly received by the prophets, even when he was persecuting the holy David, and he prophesied when the spirit of God had been made in him[3] and unwillingly proclaimed what the Apostle says, that 'truly God is in you'.[4] Those who seek to take away their property are also received by the monks living like prophets, just as we have heard from certain men, that those who had come to plunder, or who lived by robbery, having seen the humility of their life, either remained as monks or, acknowledging themselves to be unworthy of attaining such gifts, retired peacefully to their own lands. They work at whatever their superiors order them to do with such good will that it could rightly be said of them that no trace

---

[1] 4 Kgs. 1: 8. [2] Cf. Jerome, *In Esaiam*, v, 20 (*CC*, lxxiii. 201).
[3] 1 Kgs. 19: 20. [4] Cf. Phil. 2: 13, etc.

27 transeat uirtutis uestigium. Intuere mecum etiam dominum
meum Iesum, si forte alicubi tale aliquid uel huic simile fecerit.
Dicit euangelium, quia 'facta die egressus ibat in desertum
locum, et turbae requirebant eum'.¹ Dicit et alibi: 'Factum est
autem in diebus illis, exiuit in montem orare, et erat pernoctans
in oratione Dei.'² Primo intuendum est quid sit hoc, quod 'facta
die egressus ibat in desertum locum, et turbae requirebant eum,
et uenerunt usque ad ipsum', et si forte monachorum a turbis
seggregatorum uitae hoc factum domini Iesu possimus inflectere.
Ante enim ab euangelista describuntur morborum et febrium
in socru Petri et aliorum curationes, necnon demonum dicentium
'quia tu es filius Dei' expulsiones, et hoc 'cum sol occidisset',³ et
post mane facto iter eius in desertum describitur. Quid ergo sunt
febres quibus meus Iesus imperauit, qui morbi quos curauit,
quae demonia quae eiecit, nisi incentiua uitiorum quae respectu
suo et iussu extinguit, curando medetur, ne non bene sanata
iterum putrefiant, et spiritus maligni iterum in corde peccatoris
per incuriam nidificent? Hoc maxime conuenit monacho, ut
purificatus ab his, cum Iesu facto sibi die id est illuminato corde
in desertum exeat, turbam uitiorum penitus et illius mundi qui
in maligno positus est consortium simul et dominium relinquat,
ut postea proficiens et non iam sui curam solum sed etiam aliorum
habere sufficiens, a turbis pro iniquitate sua turbatis et quid
faciemus inquirentibus requiratur, et retentus dicat, 'quia et
aliis ciuitatibus oportet me euangelizare regnum Dei',⁴ id est
aliis turbis uel aliis ouibus quae adhuc non sunt de monachorum
ouili et futurae sunt, conuenit dicere, ut se suosque sequaces
imitentur. Sic enim cum Antonio interiorem heremi partem
penetrabit, ubi et angelorum contra demones auxilia, et hominum
28 se propter Deum sequentium consortia habere merebitur. Intuere
adhuc si non illud etiam implebit, quod superius de euangelio ab
Iesu factum posuimus, 'factum est autem in diebus illis, exiuit

27 of virtue escapes them. Consider with me my Lord Jesus to see whether perhaps He did this or anything like it anywhere. The Gospel says: 'When it was day, going out he went into a desert place, and the multitudes sought him.'[1] And it says elsewhere: 'And it came to pass in those days that he went out into a mountain to pray, and he passed the whole night in the prayer of God.'[2] First one must consider the meaning of 'when it was day, going out he went into a desert place, and the multitudes sought him and came to him'; and see perhaps if we can apply the sense of this action of the Lord Jesus to the life of monks separated from the multitudes. For earlier the Evangelist describes the curing of diseases and fevers in Peter's mother-in-law and others, including the expulsions of devils saying 'Thou art the Son of God', and this was 'when the sun was down',[3] and later when it was morning, His journey into the desert is described. What are the fevers my Jesus ordered cured, what were the diseases He cured, which were the demons He expelled unless they were the provokers of vice, which He extinguishes by His glance and command, remedies by His cure, lest those which are not well healed should putrefy again and evil spirits should again make their home in the heart of the sinner because of neglect? It is most fitting for a monk that, purified from these things, he should go out into the desert with Jesus when it is day for him, that is when his heart has been illuminated, should relinquish the multitude of vices entirely and the company and power of that world which is set in evil, so that, setting out afterwards and now no longer caring for himself alone but also having enough care for others, he is sought by the multitudes who are disquieted by their own iniquity, inquiring 'what shall we do', and being detained should say: 'To other cities also I must preach the kingdom of God',[4] that is to other multitudes or other sheep, who are as yet not of the flock of monks but will be of them, it is fitting to say, so that they should imitate him and his followers. For thus he will penetrate the innermost part of the desert with Anthony, where he will merit the aid of angels against demons and the company of men 28 following him for God's sake. See now if he will also fulfil what was done by Jesus, as we quoted above from the Gospel: 'And it came to pass in those days that he went into the mountain to

---

[1] Luke 4: 42.   [2] Luke 6: 12.
[3] Luke 4: 38–41.   [4] Luke 4: 43.

in montem orare, et erat pernoctans in oratione Dei.'[1] Hic etiam
inspiciendum est, quo ordine hoc fecerit. Nam ante hoc factum,
in sabbato Iesus hominem qui habebat manum aridam curauit,
et ante inutilem ad bene operandum laxauit, ut profecto ostenderet
et a malis operibus feriandum, tanquam in sabbato, et rursus ad
bene operandum manus omnes id est operationes debere extendi.
Vnde et illi homini qui sanatus est dicitur, 'extende manum
tuam',[2] id est ad bona opera a quibus sabbatizabas te exerce.
Cum uero bene operatus fueris, tunc cum Iesu in monte est
exeundum ad orationem, et ibi pernoctandum in oratione Dei
in excelso mentis quasi in monte positus excelsum Deum sequatur,
et exiens a corporalibus ad summa et caelestia rapiatur, et ibi
pernoctans, id est in tota uita sua manens, quae bonis omnibus
respectu supernae lucis non dies sed nox est, semper ut exuatur
a corpore expectet et oret. Sic enim cum patre suo et magistro
Benedicto totum mundum ante se positum quasi paruam speram
29 intuebitur, et in uisione conditoris cum ipso dilatabitur.[3] Sit
autem in huiusmodi seruis Christi sicut esse confidimus fundamentum uerae humilitatis firmum et solidum, ut quantum Christo
qui est fundamentum totius aecclesiae propinquiores esse cre-
duntur, tanto magis humilientur, ne forte super harenam collocati
facili impulsu inundantium temptationum ruant, sed Christo
inherentes et cum Christo lapides fortes caelestis edificii facti
alios inualidiores et infirmiores portare sufficiant. Obseruabunt
autem ut credimus quia serui Dei sunt, ne alterius ordinis aecclesiastici uiros licet minus ualidi sint despiciant, nec alta de se
sapient, sed humilibus consentient.[4]

IV. *De monachis qui seculares dicuntur, quorum professio nulla est.*

30 De monachis autem qui dicuntur seculares quid dicam non inuenio,
quia nec professionem monachi sequuntur, nec eorum uita us-
quam describitur. Ex magistrorum enim negligentia et ex rerum
copia et aliquando etiam inopia, magis haec uita incrementum

pray, and he passed the whole night in prayer of God.'[1] Here one must inquire in what order He did this. For before Jesus did this, He cured the man with the withered arm on the sabbath, and He loosed the previously useless member for good work, so that He might truly show both that a holiday must be taken from evil works, as if on the sabbath, and that again every man's hand should be stretched out to do good, that is works. For this reason it is also said to the man who was healed: 'Stretch forth thy hand',[2] that is exert yourself in good works from which you were taking a holiday. When you have done well, you must then go out with Jesus into the mountain to pray and pass the night there in prayer of God in the heights of your mind, as if a man, placed on a mountain, were to follow the highest God and, leaving corporeal things, be snatched up to the highest and most celestial, and spending the night there, that is staying there all his life, which concerning every good thing of the supernal light is not day but night, waits constantly and prays that he may be freed from his body. For such a man will, as his father and master Benedict did, see the whole world set before him like a tiny sphere, and in the vision of the Creator will be enlarged with him.[3] May there be in such servants of God, as we trust, a foundation of true humility, firm and solid, so that as they are believed to be nearer Christ, Who is the foundation of the whole church, may they be the more humble, lest perhaps, built on sand, they be ruined by the swift shock of a flood of temptations, but, clinging to Christ and made with Christ strong stones of a heavenly building, may they become strong enough to support others weaker and feebler. They will take care, we believe, since they are God's servants, not to look down on other orders of men in the church, even though they are less strong, not think themselves higher, but will feel united with the humble.[4]

IV. *Monks who are called seculars, who take no vows.*

I do not know what to say about the monks who are called seculars, since they do not follow the monks' way of life and the life they do follow is nowhere described. From the negligence of masters and from the plentifulness of things at some times, and the shortage

---

[1] Luke 6: 12.   [2] Luke 6: 10.
[3] Gregory, *Dial.*, II, 35 (ed. Moricca, p. 129).
[4] Rom. 12: 16.

accepit. Contingit enim aliquando ut rerum affluentia disso-
lutionem pariat, et dum nichil temporale deest, sollicitudo et
animi fortitudo protinus abest. Euenit etiam sepe, ut cum in
abbatis manu necessaria desunt quae monachis dentur, non audeat
eos pro dissolutione aliqua uel delicto redarguere, et ita fit, ut cum
terrena a monachis inordinate quaeruntur, ordinis districtio et
aeternorum premiorum cura relinquatur. Bene igitur facient
utrique si se corrigant, si nomen monachi quod portant honorent.

V. *De canonicis qui longe se ab hominibus constituunt, ut sunt*
  Premonstrenses, et SanctiIudocenses.[1]

31 Igitur de monachis paucis pro uiribus premissis, ad canonicos
ueniendum est, quorum ordo refrigescente multorum caritate
quondam tepuerat, sed nostra aetate gratia Dei aliquantulum
iam refloruit. Cuius autem auctoritatis sit eorum ordo et professio,
Domino donante pro posse ostendere temptabimus. Primum
igitur intuendum est, quod iste ordo iam tripertitus habeatur,
ita ut alii a turbis omnino conuersatione et habitu et habitatione
quantum possunt seggregentur, alii iuxta homines positi sint,
alii inter homines habitent, unde et seculares appellantur. Videndum
est etiam, quid canonici nomen insinuet. Canon enim intelligitur
regula, et canonicus dicitur regularis. Vnde autem hic ordo initium
sumpsit? An forte ab apostolis? Et hoc ex parte uerum est, quia
sicut illi debent communiter uiuere, et nichil proprium possidere.
Sed est quod altius perscrutari possit. Ipsorum est enim populos
docere, decimas accipere, oblata in domo Domini suscipere,
delinquentes redarguere, correctos et paenitentes aecclesiae
reconciliare, et alia quae etiam in lege antiquitus obseruabantur,
etiam nunc in aecclesia nostri temporis obseruare. Legamus in
libro numerorum, si forte inuenire poterimus in eo canonicorum
pretentam speciem. Describuntur enim in illo libro officia
leuitarum, quos Deus assumpsisse se dicit de medio filiorum

of them at others, this way of life is becoming more and more common. For it sometimes happens that affluence produces dissoluteness, and when nothing temporal is lacking, solicitude and strength of spirit always are. It also often happens that when the abbot does not have those necessary things which should be given to the monks, he does not dare upbraid them for their faults of lack of discipline, and similarly it happens that when earthly things are sought excessively by monks, the strictness of the order and care for eternal rewards are abandoned. They will both therefore benefit by putting this to rights, if they would honour the name of monk which they bear.

V. *Canons who establish themselves far from men, such as the Premonstratensians and the canons of Saint-Josse.*[1]

1 Having mentioned so far as I am able these few things about monks, I must now come to the canons. Their order, when the charity of many was cooling, formerly became tepid, but in our day, thanks be to God, it has now begun to flourish somewhat. We shall try to show from whose authority they take their order and way of life, God willing. One must first understand that this order has three parts now: some are separated from the multitudes entirely by their way of life and habit and dwelling-place as much as possible; others are situated next to men; and others live among men and are thus called seculars. One must first see what the name canon implies. For canon means rule, and to be a canon means to live under a rule. How then did this order begin? Perhaps with the apostles? This is partly true, since like them they have to live communally and own no property. But there is something which could be scrutinized more profoundly. Their task is to teach the people, take tithes, collect offerings in church, remonstrate with delinquents, reconcile the corrected and penitent to the church, and observe other duties also laid down in the old law which are still kept in the church of our day. Let us read in the book of Numbers to see whether we shall find in it by chance anything similar to the canons' claims. The duties of the levites are described in this book, whom God said He had taken up from

[1] The Premonstratensian abbey of Saint-Josse-au-Bois was founded in 1120 and moved in 1161 to Dommartin in the present diocese of Arras: Albéric de Calonne, *Histoire des abbayes de Dommartin et de Saint-André-au-Bois* (Arras, 1875), pp. 4 and 14.

Israel pro primogenitis eorum,[1] ut in tabernaculo eius ministrarent,
de quibus erat et summus pontifex. Describitur etiam quid
Gersonitae agere debeant, quid Caathitae, quid filii Merari, et
quidam eorum in tabernaculo federis intrare dicuntur, coram
summo pontifice, et inuoluta portare,[2] et alii cortinas et operimentum et tentorium, et 'omnia quae pertinent ad altare, funiculos
et uasa ministerii',[3] et alii 'tabulas tabernaculi et uectes eius,
columpnas et bases earum, columpnas atrii cum basibus et
paxillis et funibus, et omnia uasa et supellectilem'.[4] Si de omnibus
his uel aliis quae ibi scribuntur rationem reddere uoluerimus,
tenuitas ingenioli deficiet. Vnde ad sanctos doctores lectorem
horum remittimus. Vnum tantum est ut intelligatur, quia sicut
in ueteri lege leuitarum erat officium sanctificata custodire, et
ferre, et mundare, sic et in hoc tempore canonicorum esse credo
similia agere, nec quemquam ad ministerium aecclesiae debere
admitti, nisi qui regulariter et honeste uixerit, quod nomine
ipso canonici indicatur. Sicut enim in ueteri lege leuitis uiuendi
est regula prescripta, quis quid[a] agere debeat, nec ad aliud uacare
licebat, nisi ad quod erat ordinatus, nec aliis licebat eorum officia
tractare, ita credo et in hoc tempore faciendum esse. Videamus
ergo si forte in his tribus familiis leuitici ordinis tripertitum
ordinem canonicorum inuenire ualeamus, seposita summi pontificis familia, quae huius temporis summum pontificem et episcopos
sine dubio prefigurabat, et potestatem et dignitatem eorum pre-
tendebat. Primum igitur de illis canonicis loquamur, secundum
lectionis numeri significationem, qui longius ab hominibus secedunt, et actu et uita et conuersatione quantum possunt ab eis
longe se faciunt, ut liberius Deo ministrent. Inspiciamus igitur
officia Caathitarum, qui a summo pontifice et filiis eius archam
testamenti et altare aureum et candelabrum et mensam et digniora
uasa inuoluta portare iubentur, et sanctuario interiori post familiam
summi pontificis propinquius quam Gersonitae et Meraritae
deseruiunt, ita ut intrent in interiori sanctuario, et inuoluta a

---

[a] quid quis *corr.* quis quid

among the sons of Israel in place of their firstborn,[1] so that they should serve in His tabernacle, of whom He was also the highest pontiff. There is described what the Gersonites were to do, the Caathites, the sons of Merari, and some of them are said to enter the tabernacle of the covenant in the presence of the high priest to carry the cover thereof,[2] and others the curtains and the covering and the hanging and 'all things that pertain to the altar, the cords and the vessels of the ministry',[3] and others 'the boards of the tabernacle and the bars thereof, the pillars and their sockets, the pillars of the court with their sockets and the pins and cords and all the vessels and furniture'.[4] If we should wish to give a meaning to all these matters and others which are described here, the thinness of my poor wit would not be adequate. For this we send the reader of these things to the sacred doctors. Only one thing is to be understood, that just as in the old law it was the duty of the levites to look after the sacred objects, and carry them and clean them, so in our day I believe the canons are to carry out similar tasks, and no one should be admitted to the ministry of the church unless he has lived purely and in accordance with a rule, which is indicated by the very name of canon. For just as in the old law the levites' rule of life is prescribed, who should do what, and that a man should not have time for any other task unless he has been ordained to it, and that others should not do their duties, so I believe this should also be done in our day. Let us see then if we can find perhaps in these three levitical families the three-part order of canons, leaving aside the family of the high priest, who doubtless prefigured the supreme pontiff and the bishops of our day and laid claim to their power and dignity. First let us speak of those canons, according to the meaning of the lesson in Numbers, who withdraw far from men and who conduct their activity, life, and discipline as far away from them as they can in order more freely to serve God. Let us therefore examine the duties of the Caathites, who were ordered by the high priest and his sons to carry the ark of the covenant and the golden altar and candlestick and the table and the more worthy covered vessels, and who are closest to the inner sanctuary after the family of the high priest, which the Gersonites and the Merarites serve, so that they may enter the inner sanctuary and take up and carry those things

32

---

[1] Num. 3: 12.   [2] Num. 4: 15.
[3] Num. 4: 25–6.   [4] Num. 4: 31–2.

summo pontifice uel filiis eius portanda suscipiant. Isti ergo filii
Caath quanto propinquiores erant interiori sanctuario, tanto
longe fiebant a populo. Vnde non immerito his comparantur
canonici illi, qui sicut leuitae illi officia aecclesiastica suscipiunt,
et longe ab hominibus secedentes, propinquius sanctuarii interioris
uasa, id est, contemplatiuae uitae gaudia secum uehunt. Quibus
etiam Caathitarum nomen conuenit. Caath enim interpretatur
paenitens, siue dolens.[1] Tales enim prius compunguntur timore,
postea amore, et de factis suis malis primum paenitentes, et
ueraciter flentes, postmodum a triginta annis et supra, id est, a
perfectione uirtutis et credulitate sanctae trinitatis in aecclesia
sacros ordines suscipiunt, ut bene meritos quinquagesimus annus
suscipiat, et liberati a uoluptatibus carnis uasa dominica non
onerati humeris deferant, sed iustificati et probati custodiant.
33 Est etiam in his secundum lectionis numeri tenorem ordo dis-
pertitus, ut a summo pontifice diuidatur unicuique onus quod
portare quis debeat. Vnde conicere possumus, quod quidam
eorum sanctiora pro sanctitate uitae portanda suscipiebant, et
alii qui minus ualidi in uirtutibus habebantur minoribus officiis
deputabantur. Eadem enim familia quae altare aureum et candelabrum et mensam et ipsam etiam archam portabat, in sequentibus
iacinctinas pelles et uectes et lucernas et forcipes et emunctoria
portare perhibetur, necnon fuscinulas, et tridentes, uncinos et
batilla. Intuere ergo, quod similis forma in ordinibus canonicorum
qui longe ab hominibus secedunt iam custodiatur, quando et
ipsi de populo Dei tanquam leuitae assumpti, non aequaliter
sacros ordines suscipiunt, sed aliqui eorum ad ministerium
sacerdotale attolluntur, aliqui ad diaconatus officium promouentur,
nonnulli ad subdiaconatus gradum assciscuntur, aliqui etiam in
acolitorum, exorcistarum, hostiariorum, lectorum, ordine de-
putantur, uel ad extremum alii minus ad haec agenda idonei in
aecclesia tantum ad clericatum suscipiuntur, unde etiam inter
suos conuersi apellantur.[2] Qui uero in suo ordine profecerit,

which have been wrapped by the high priest or his sons. Therefore the nearer these sons of Caath were to the inner sanctuary, the further they were from the people. For which reason they can be compared not inappropriately to those canons who take up their offices in the church like levites and withdrawing far from men take the vessels with them nearer to the inner sanctuary, that is carry with them the joys of the contemplative life. For these the name of the Caathites is fitting, since Caath means penitent or grieving.[1] Such men, moved first by fear and then by love, and first feeling penitence for their evil deeds and truly lamenting them, after they are thirty years old or more, that is by the perfection of virtue and belief in the Holy Trinity, receive holy orders in the church, so that the fiftieth year finds them well deserving and freed from the pleasures of the flesh, and they do not carry the vessels of the Lord as a burden on their shoulders but guard them, justified and tested. Further, according to the lesson in Numbers, duties are assigned within the order and the high priest decides which person must bear which burden. And so we may assume that some men used to take up certain duties in accordance with the holiness of their life, and others less advanced in virtue had lesser duties assigned to them. For the very family which carried the golden altar and the candlestick and table and even the ark itself was assigned next to carry also the violet skins and bars, and lamps and tongs and snuffers, and also the flesh-hooks and forks, pot-hooks and shovels. Note therefore that a similar plan is observed now in the orders of canons, who withdraw far from men, for even though they are taken from God's people like the levites, they do not receive holy orders equally. Some are assigned to the priestly ministry, some are promoted to the office of deacon, some are admitted to the grade of subdeacon, and others are deputed to be acolytes, exorcists, door-keepers, and lectors, and, finally, others less suitable for these tasks are taken into the church simply as clerics, whence they are called among themselves *conversi*.[2] Whoever has truly progressed in his rank, who in the

[1] Jerome, *Nom. heb.* (*CC*, lxxii. 74 and n. 17).
[2] On the significance of the order of the grades listed here (and on pp. 10–12), see introd., p. xxi; on *conversi* in the canonical order, see C. D. Fonseca, 'I conversi nelle comunità canonicali', in *I laici*, pp. 262–305, with full references to earlier literature on this topic and on lay brothers generally. From this passage it is clear that the author of the *Libellus* regarded *conversi* as clerics, and presumably tonsured, although in no grade of holy orders.

seniorum iudicio qui ante in minori ordine locatus fuerat ab episcopo tanquam ab Eleazaro[a] maiorem ordinem suscipit.

34 Preter haec etiam officia quae ab uniuersali aecclesia exposcuntur, sicut in ordinibus dicitur, quod non illa aut illa aecclesia hoc exposcat, sed postulat sancta mater aecclesia,[1] sunt alia officia quae pro uitae merito unicuique distribuuntur, ut inde seruiant non uniuersali aecclesiae, sed fratribus suis et hospitibus et peregrinis, ueluti est quod unus eligitur in abbatem, alter subrogatur in priorem, alter in elemosinarium uel coquinarium, uel cellararium, et ut ad uiliora descendam, alter alendis peccoribus deputatur, ut impleatur in eis etiam illud quod scribitur de Caathitis: 'Filiis autem Caath non dedit plaustra et boues, quia in sanctuario seruiunt, et cara propriis portant humeris.'[2] Sic et canonici qui longe ab hominibus secedunt propriis humeris onera portant, cum et spiritualia quibusque seruis Dei ministrant, et in carnalibus sibi ipsis ministrantes, uictum sibi de manibus acquirunt. Onera propriis portant humeris, cum et Deo militant, in eius sanctuario id est in sancta aecclesia seruientes, et quasi utrobique fortes, et iugum Christi portant, nec a fidelibus decimas uel redditus quod sacerdotum uel canonicorum clericorumue est extorquent, licet aliquando data suscipiant, illos profecto imitantes, qui accepta potestate uiuendi de euangelio quod predicabant,[3]

35 laborabant tamen manibus suis, ne quem grauarent.[4] Intuere etiam dominum Iesum si aliquid egerit simile, et si forte quicquam quod canonicorum talium factis assimiletur, aliquo actu perpetrauerit. Et quia tales canonicos filiis Caath comparauimus, qui tamen ex ordine minorum sacerdotum erant preter summi pontificis familiam, non indignum uideatur si utrisque Iesus noster comperaretur, 'qui minoratus est' etiam paulominus ab angelis,[5] et 'didicit ex his quae passus est obaedientiam',[6] ut esset sicut Caathitae non in se sed in membris suis sub Eleazaro filio summi

---

[a] Eleazero *corr.* Eleazaro

judgement of his superiors has been placed previously in a lower rank, receives a higher one from his bishop, as if from Eleazar. And over and above these duties which are required by the universal church—as is said in the orders of service, this or that church does not request this, but holy mother church demands it,[1]—there are other duties which are assigned according to each person's merits so that they will serve thereby not the universal church but their brothers, guests, and pilgrims, just as when one man is elected abbot, another is made his deputy as prior, another is put in the almonry or kitchen or cellar, and, descending to the lowest, another is made herdsman, so that it may be fulfilled in them as was written of the Caathites: 'But to the sons of Caath he gave no wagons or oxen; because they serve in the sanctuary and carry the precious things upon their shoulders.'[2] So too do the canons, who withdraw from men, carry burdens upon their own shoulders, when they minister to God's servants spiritually and to themselves carnally, by earning their livelihood by their own labours. They carry their burdens on their own shoulders also when they fight for God in His sanctuary, that is by serving in the holy church, and strong as it were in both, they carry Christ's yoke too. They do not exact tithes and rents from the faithful, which the priests and canons and clerics do, though sometimes they accept whatever is given them, imitating perfectly those who, having accepted the power of living by the Gospel which they preach,[3] nevertheless laboured with their hands lest they be a burden to anyone.[4] See if the Lord Jesus did anything like this and if any of His acts can be compared to such things done by the canons. And since we have compared such canons to the sons of Caath, who however were from a minor order of priests, except the family of the high priest, it does not seem unsuitable if the Lord Jesus is compared to either, who was also made a little lower than the angels[5] and 'learned obedience by the things which he suffered',[6] so that He should be like the Caathites not in Himself but in His members, under Eleazar, the son of the high priest,

---

[1] Cyrille Vogel and Reinhard Elze, *Le Pontifical romano-germanique du dixième siècle* (Studi e testi, 226–7; Rome, 1963) i. 14, ll. 5–6.

[2] Num. 7: 9.   [3] 1 Cor. 9: 14.

[4] On the refusal of the more austere type of monks and canons to own tithes and other clerical revenues and their determination to live in solitude and work with their hands, see Constable, *Tithes*, p. 155 (and *passim*).

[5] Heb. 2: 9.   [6] Heb. 5: 8.

sacerdotis, qui interpretatur 'Deus adiutor meus'.[1] Pergens
igitur ad passionem susceptus est a Iudeis, et[a] eductus, 'et baiulans
sibi crucem, exiuit in eum qui dicitur Caluariae locum, hebraice
Golgotha, ubi eum crucifixerunt'.[2] Primum uide ordinem, quem
etiam hic obseruauit Iesus. Nam et familia Caath ut supradictum
est in maiores et minores sacerdotes diuisa erat, et pontifex summus
ex eadem erat familia. Sic et Iesus fecit, 'obaediens existens patri
usque ad mortem, mortem autem crucis',[3] prius portauit crucem
sibi quasi filii Caath altare aureum, ut ipse dignus existens summo
sacerdotio, postea aram illam crucis omni auro et omni mundo
preciosiorem ascenderet, ut dolens pro nobis et 'uulneratus
propter scelera nostra',[4] taliter gradu summi sacerdotii iuste
potiretur, et acciperet 'nomen quod est super omne nomen'.[5]

36 Tu ergo qui canonicus es, et ob uitae et professionis tuae decorem
longe te ab hominibus faciens, et propter hoc forsitan in sanctuario
propinquius ministrans, uis gradatim uel uirtutes Iesu uel aecclesiastica sacramenta suscipere, ut ordo familiae canonicalis
exposcit, imitare et intuere Iesum meum non subito summa
petentem, sed gradatim ad summa tendentem.[6] Porta tibi cum
illo crucem et ipsum sequere,[7] et 'carnem' tuam si Christi es
'cum uitiis et concupiscentiis crucifige',[8] et exiens cum illo 'extra
castra'[9] totum te in Caluariae loco cruci affige, et quasi caluus
totum caput id est principale illud mentis tuae a terrenis habens
denudatum 'improperium eius' portare gaudeto.[9] Taliter etiam
conueniet tibi nomen Caath, qui alia interpretatione dicitur
molares dentes uel patientia.[10] Ruminans enim dentibus interioris
hominis tui uerbum Dei et confringens subtiliter ut possis illud
gluttire et memoriae commendare,[11] patientiam habens erga

---

[a] et *add. supra*

which means 'God is my help'.[1] Proceeding therefore to His
passion, He was taken by the Jews and led out 'and bearing his
own cross he went forth to the place which is called Calvary, in
Hebrew Golgotha, where they crucified him'.[2] First observe the
order which Jesus kept even here. For the family of Caath, as
was said above, was divided into major and minor priests and the
high priest was from the same family. This also Jesus did, obedient
to His father 'unto death, even to the death of the cross'.[3] First
He carried His cross, as the sons of Caath did the golden altar, so
that being worthy as high priest He should later ascend the altar
of the cross, which is more precious than all gold and the whole
world; and grieving for us and 'wounded for our sins',[4] He should
justly obtain the rank of high priest and take 'a name which is
above all names'.[5] You therefore who are a canon, and because of
your vows and way of life live far from men, and because of this
perhaps serving more closely the sanctuary, you wish gradually
to take on either the powers of Jesus or the sacraments of the
church, as the order of the canonical family urges, to imitate and
contemplate my Jesus, not seeking the heights at once but tending
gradually thither.[6] Carry your cross with Him and follow Him,[7]
and if you are Christ's, crucify your flesh 'with the vices and
concupiscences'[8] and going forth with Him 'without the camp'[9]
nail yourself wholly to the cross in Calvary, and as if with a
completely shaven head, that is having denuded the principal
part of your mind of worldly things, rejoice in bearing His
reproach.[9] So much will the name of Caath fit you, for by another
interpretation it means molar teeth or patience.[10] Chewing the
cud, the word of God, with the teeth of your interior man
and subtly grinding it down so finely that you can swallow it and
commit it to memory,[11] having patience for your detractors and

---

[1] Jerome, *Nom. heb.* (*CC*, lxxii. 74).   [2] John 19:17–18.
[3] Phil. 2: 8.   [4] Isa. 53: 5.   [5] Phil. 2: 9.
[6] Cf. on this passage G. G. Meersseman, 'Eremitismo e predicazione itinerante dei secoli XI e XII', *Eremitismo*, p. 167 (and n. 11), who stressed the
importance to St. Norbert and the austere orders of canons of the concept of a
slow, progressive rise to the priesthood as a means of raising the level of the
diocesan clergy, and who compared the idea expressed here of gradually
receiving the powers of Jesus and the ecclesiastical sacraments to the orders of
Christ mentioned pp. 10–12 and 60 above (and introd., p. xxi).
[7] Matt. 10: 38; 16: 24; etc.   [8] Gal. 5: 24.   [9] Heb. 13: 13.
[10] Jerome, *Nom. heb.* (*CC*, lxxii. 74).
[11] On the comparison of monks to ruminants in the Middle Ages, cf. Leclercq,
Vocabulaire, pp. 136–7.

detractores et persequutores, et findens ungulam benignus in
Deum benignus in proximum, et ruminans Dei uerbum[1] non
sicut stultus qui degluttit illud ita mundum animal fies, et Iesu
Christi comedens carnem et sanguinem bibens mutaberis in
37 ipso, et membrum corporis eius efficieris. Quod si quis obiciat
et dicat Caathitas etiam aliis canonicis uel sacerdotibus uel ministris
posse comparari, et rursum dominum Iesum crucem sibi baiulan-
tem omnibus fidelibus suis qui crucem eius in se portant posse
conferri, et ego consentio, et haec dicentem, approbo. Sed non
cuiquam graue debet uideri, si illum propinquiorem sanctuario
interiori iudico, qui maiorem laborem pro Christo assumpsit,
uel si illum paulo amplius Christo consimilem quam me in eius
cruce portanda dixerim, qui maiorem quam ego oneris illius
piissimi partem arripuit. Cum enim me amplius uigilant, ieiunant,
laborant, algent, et ut ad digniora ueniam, cum humiliores et
pauperiores pro Christo sunt, sub sarcina illa piissima quasi
altiores et fortiores[a] in medio curuatos intueor, me autem cum
ipsis sub ipsa sarcina quasi humiliore humeros submisisse et[b]
manus posuisse et brachia tentendisse ut infirmior quod possem
facerem aspicio. Sunt enim ipsi tales, qui humilitatem integre et
pure custodiant, ita ut quae uiliora sunt pro fratribus agant,
stabula ut audiuimus mundantes, et caetera contemptibilium
seruorum officia perficientes. Non enim dedignantur stabula uel
boum asinorumque presepia mundare, cum legant in euangelio
Dominum suum propter nos in presepio dignatum iacere.[2]
Sectantur etiam et ipsi tantam circa aduentantes hospitalitatem,
et humanitatem, ut Habrahae et Loth consimiles iure dicantur,
qui aliquando angelos susceperunt, quia hospites dilexerunt.[3]
Habent etiam in uictu et uestitu tantam austeritatem, ut Iohannem
Baptistam imitari uideantur, qui natus de sacerdotali stirpe
consortia secularium fugiebat, et 'pilis cameli zonaque pellicea'
uestiebatur, 'et mel siluestre' comedebat.[4] Ne uero per multi-
loquium peccatum incurrant, iuge silentium tenere, uel pauca
loqui dicuntur, ut cultum iusticiae omnino sequantur. Laudo
professionis huius magnanimitatem, predico erga corpus austeritatem, amo tantam eorum humilitatem, sed modum in omnibus

---

    [a] altiores et fortiores *add. supra*   [b] quasi . . . et *add. supra*

persecutors, and, dividing your hoof, benign in God and benign in your neighbour; chewing the cud on the word of God,[1] not as a fool who bolts it down, you will become like the clean animal, and eating the flesh and drinking the blood of Jesus Christ, you will change into Him and become a member of His body. If anyone should object and say that the Caathites can be compared also with other canons, or priests, or ministers, and again that the Lord Jesus bearing His cross can be compared with all the faithful bearing His cross on themselves, I must agree and assent to what they say. But it ought not to seem a serious matter to anyone if I judge a man who takes up a greater labour for Christ to be nearer the inner sanctuary, or if I say that he is a little more like Christ than I in carrying His cross, he who has taken hold of a greater part of that most pious burden than I have. Since they watch, fast, labour, and brave the elements more than I, and, to come to more important things, are among those who are more humble and poor for Christ, I regard those men bowed under that most pious burden before all eyes as higher and stronger, and I see myself, having put my shoulders with them under that burden and positioned my hands and stretched out my arms in a more lowly fashion, in order, being weaker, to do what I can. For they are such men as guard their humility with integrity and purity, doing more ignominious things for their brothers, cleaning stables, as I have heard, and performing other tasks of the lower servants. They do not disdain to clean out the stables or mangers of cattle or asses, since they read in the Gospel that their Lord was deemed worthy to lie in a manger for our sake.[2] They also take pains to provide such hospitality and kindness for guests that they are rightly said to be similar to Abraham and Lot, who used to receive angels since they loved guests.[3] They also observe such austerity in their food and clothing that they seem to imitate John the Baptist, who, born of a priestly race, would flee the company of the world and dress himself in camel hair and a leather girdle and eat wild honey.[4] Lest they should incur sin through loquacity, they are said to keep silence continually or to speak but little and to follow the cult of righteousness entirely. I praise the magnanimity of this way of life; I preach austerity towards the body; I love their great humility; but I declare there is a measure

---

[1] Cf. Deut. 14: 6.   [2] Luke 2: 7.
[3] Gen. 19: 1.   [4] Matt. 3: 4.

tenendum esse pronuntio. Cum enim audio sacerdotes et ipsum etiam abbatem in hoc ordine canonicorum, qui longe uita et conuersatione a secularibus se faciunt, et in illo etiam ordine monachorum qui similiter secedunt de quo superius tractauimus lac de ouibus suis mulgere, stabula mundare, uix possum credere, sed tamen cum hoc uel tandem credo, humilitatem eorum ueneror et admiror. Video enim illos haec ideo agere, ut superbia in eis omnino confundatur, et humilitas erigatur. Vellem tamen eos qui circa altare cotidie ministrant, et maxime illos qui cotidie pro officio sacerdotii corpus Christi tractant ob reuerentiam ipsius corporis quo nichil mundius esse potest ista non agere, sed aliis qui ad illa officia suscipienda in aecclesia adhuc idonei non sunt, haec agenda relinquere. Nam et in libro numerorum de quo superius aliqua memorauimus cum secundum Dei preceptum tribus leuitica numeraretur, et 'ab uno mense et supra' numerus ipse inciperet, et usque ad uiginti duo milia surgeret,[1] tamen non sunt inuenti 'a triginta annis et supra usque ad .L. annum, nisi octo milia quingenti octoginta',[2] qui ad ministerium tabernaculi uel altaris possent assumi. Quid igitur de his qui minores natu erant dicemus? Nichilne illi qui annorum erant quindecim seu uiginti egisse dicendi sunt? Credo et illos et credendum est uirtutum habuisse exercitia, ut in minoribus probati, et exercitati, decimas frustra non comederent, sed patribus suis obaedientes et humiliter obsequentes illis laxatis ab officio, unusquisque pro uitae merito patri succederet. Ita et hic potest fieri, ut si sunt aliqui fratres in aecclesia qui ad illa sancta tractanda adhuc minus idonei sint, in istis quae humilitatem exerceant et superbiam frangant exerceantur, ut postea emeritis senibus quiescentibus et uasa id est ministros ipsos uel fideles quosque custodientibus iure succedant. Illi uero sua officia quae mundiciam maxime expetunt, in omnibus honorent. Quod si michi dicat aliquis quia 'omnia munda mundis',[3] et ego faueo, sed requiro utrum indumenta illa quibus ad altare accedunt munda etiam exterius esse debeant, uel qua cura corporalia et mantilia seu manutergia tractanda sint. Si uero munda ea esse oportet sicut etiam in

to be held to in everything. When I hear of priests and even an abbot in this order of canons, who lead their life and profession far from worldly things, and also in that order of monks who withdraw similarly, of whom we have written above, milking their own ewes and cleaning stables, I can hardly believe it; but nevertheless since I do believe it at long last, I venerate their humility and wonder at it. For I see them do these things in such a way that pride is completely confounded in them and humility is

38 encouraged. I could wish, however, that those who serve the altar every day, and especially those who offer the body of Christ every day during their duties as priests, did not engage in such work, out of reverence for His body, since nothing can be cleaner; but they should leave it to others who are not yet suited for the assumption of such duties in the church. For in the book of Numbers, of which we have spoken somewhat above, when the tribes of the levites were numbered according to God's command, and He began from the age of 'one month and upwards' and went up to twenty-two thousand,[1] nevertheless there were found 'from thirty years old and upward until fifty years old only eight thousand five hundred and eighty'[2] who could be taken for the service of the altar or the tabernacle, and what then shall we say of those who were younger? Are those of fifteen or twenty years of age said to have performed nothing? I believe, and it should be believed, that they too exercised the virtues, so that they were practised and tested in minor matters and did not consume tithes uselessly but, obeying their fathers and submitting to them humbly, having been released from duties by them, each should succeed to his father according to the merit of his life. This can also be done here, so that if there are any brothers in the church who are as yet less fitted for holy duties, let them be exercised in those tasks which practise humility and break down pride, so that later when their worn-out elders have retired, they may succeed rightfully as guardians of the vessels, that is the ministers and the faithful. Let them honour in every way their offices, which particularly

39 demand cleanliness. If someone should say to me that 'all things are clean to the clean',[3] I agree, but I ask whether the clothing of those who ascend the altar should also be externally clean and how should the cloths, table-cloths, and towels be cared for. If it is proper that those things should be clean, as is enjoined on

_____
[1] Num. 3: 43.   [2] Num. 4: 47–8.   [3] Tit. 1: 15.

accipiendis ordinibus subdiaconibus iniungitur ut ea munda
faciant, quantomagis manus quae corpus Christi conficiunt,
tangunt, eleuant, portant, amplectuntur, aliis tribuunt, mundae
exterius seruandae sunt? Quod si mundare eis domos placet,
habent etiam ipsi in hoc officium suum, ut mundare debeant
aecclesiae pauimenta non equorum stabula. Lege in libro
Machabeorum, ubi 'elegit Iudas sacerdotes sine macula, uoluntatem habentes in lege, et mundauerunt sancta'.¹ Sanctus etiam
Ieronimus in commentario Mathei sacerdotibus exprobrat, quod
cum 'debuissent parietes templi leuigare, pauimenta uerrere, uasa
mundare', tunc faciebant 'consilium quomodo occiderent Dominum'.² Ecce habes et in mundanis aecclesiae parietibus uel
pauimentis antiquorum exemplum, quos imitari humilitati non
erit inimicum, et munditiae reuerentiaeque, quae corpori Christi
40 etiam in exterioribus debentur non erit aduersum. Quod si dicat
aliquis ablutione aquae illas sordes supramemoratas cito mundari,
quid erit si talia inheserint quae non cito recedant, et quid de
uestimentis cotidianisᵃ cum quibus necessario ad altare acceditur,
si talibus sordibus inficiantur? Non enim cotidie possunt ipsa
mutari. Si uero dicat adhuc aliquis in interioribus non exterioribus
debere esse munditiam, et quia Iesus in regione nostra sordes
exteriores sicut famem et sitim pro nobis pati non repudiauit,
amplector quidem humilitatem, sed dico sputa Iudeorum iam
non esse in facie Iesu quae pependit in ligno, nec me tale corpus
Christi sumere quale fuit cum esset passibilis, sed tale, quale
nunc est cum sedet ad dexteram patris. Tale corpus Christi
credo, teneo, amplector, sumo, in uisceribus interioris mei traicio,
et corpus illud intus et exterius, sicut animam eius mundum
prae omni mundicia esse pronuntio, et amo circa corpus eius
uenerationem, cuius 'caro non uidit corruptionem'.³ Si autem
placet eis tanta humilitas et sui deiectio, placeat eis et meus circa
corpus Christi cultus et deuotio. Sed si pretendant nobis ex regula
sua laborem manuum sibi iniunctum, sunt multa quae cum reuer-
entia illa dominici corporis possunt exerceri, ut est fodere, ligna
41 uel segetes cedere, plantare, seminare, et his similia. Non hoc
dico quasi reprehendam eorum humilitatem quae custos est
caeterarum uirtutum, quaeque talibus indiciis propalatur, sed

ᵃ cotidianis *add. in marg.*

sub-deacons when they take orders that they should make them clean, how much more should the hands that prepare the body of Christ, touch, elevate, carry, cherish, and distribute it to others be kept clean externally? And if it pleases them to clean their houses, they also have in their duty to clean the church floor, not the stables of horses. Read in the book of Machabees, where Judas 'chose priests without blemish whose will was set upon the law of God and they cleansed the holy places'.[1] St. Jerome also in his commentary on Matthew upbraids the priests who when 'they had to scrape the walls of the temple, sweep the floors, clean the vessels', then took 'counsel as to how they might kill the Lord'.[2] There you have in the cleaning of the walls and floors of the church in ancient times examples, the imitation of which would not be inimical to humility nor against the cleanliness and reverence which are owed to the body of Christ even in externals. But if someone says that by being washed with water the dirt mentioned above is cleansed quickly, what will happen if it persists and does not quickly disappear? And what about daily clothing in which one must ascend the altar, if such dirt discolours it? That cannot be changed every day. If someone says that cleanliness should be internal not external and that Jesus did not disdain to suffer outward uncleanliness while on our earth any more than hunger and thirst, I embrace indeed his humility, but I say the spit of the Jews is not now on the face of Jesus which hung on the cross, nor do I consume the body of Christ as it was when it suffered but as it is now seated at the right hand of the Father. Such is the body of Christ I believe in, hold, embrace, consume, absorb into my innermost entrails, and I declare that body inwardly and outwardly clean as His soul above all cleanliness, and I love the veneration of His body, of which the 'flesh shall not see corruption'.[3] If then such humility and adversity on His part pleases them, let my worship and devotion for the body of Christ please them too. But if they protest to us that their rule enjoins manual labour on them, then there are many things which can be carried out with reverence for the body of the Lord, such as digging, cutting wood, and reaping crops, planting, sowing and the like. I do not say this to cast a slur upon their humility, which is the guardian of the other virtues and which is made manifest by

[1] 1 Mach. 4: 42–3.   [2] Jerome, *In Matt.*, xxvi (*PL*, xxvi. 1988).
[3] Acts 2: 31.

ostendo meam circa corpus Christi deuotionem. Ipsi uero si aliud
aliter sapiunt, hoc quoque illis Deus reuelauit. Sane de regula
illa quam plurimi canonicorum quia sic intitulatur beati Augustini
esse affirmant, non audeo certum aliquid definire. Si enim
dixero illius non esse, titulus ipse qui ubique nomen Augustini
tenet, contradicet michi.[1] Rursus si affirmare uoluero illius esse,
duo sunt quae obici possunt, et a pluribus dicuntur, quia nec in
libro Retractionum, ut eius plures libri posita est, nec modus
uerborum et stili grauitas illius Aurelii fuisse comprobat, quae in
illa regula plurimum desunt. Certius est illud, quod de uita sua
in libro Confessionum ipse ponit, quod 'factus presbyter mona-
sterium' clericorum mox 'instituit, et coepit uiuere secundum
regulam sub sanctis apostolis constitutam', et illud quod de uita
illius Possidius discipulus eius scripsit.[2] Nemo ergo pro regula
illa socium uiae Dei, esse preuaricatorem credat, quam illius
auctoris fuisse multi dubitant. Sit uero in omnibus canonicis
unus[a] affectus obseruandi quod quisque uouerit, uel quod
unusquisque in sua aecclesia quod religioni non obuiat inuenit.

VI. *De canonicis qui iuxta hominum conuersationem habitationem*[b]
  habent, ut sunt SanctiQuintinienses de prato, et
  SanctiVictorienses.[3]

42 Quoniam in superioribus post monachos diuersi habitus et ordinis
de canonicis qui longe se ab hominibus faciunt pauca pro uiribus
diximus, nunc ad illos canonicorum mores et ordinem ueniendum
est, quos quasi in medio positos inspicere possumus, ut nec sicut
illi qui longius secedunt consortia hominum mundanorum omnino

---

  [a] unus *add. supra*   [b] habitationem *add. (rep.)*

such signs, but to show my devotion to Christ's body. And surely, if some take one view and some another, they have all been guided by God. Indeed, I do not dare to explain anything certain about that rule which, since it is so entitled, has been affirmed by many canons to be by St. Augustine. If I should say that it is not by him, the very title which everywhere bears Augustine's name would contradict me.[1] On the other hand, if I should wish to affirm that it is by him, there are two objections that could be made and are put forward by many: that it is not listed in the Retractations as are most of his works and that the kind of vocabulary and gravity of style attesting to Aurelius' work are clearly missing in this rule. What is more certain is that which he wrote about his life in the Confessions and that 'when he became a priest he soon established a monastery' of clerics 'and began to live according to a rule established at the time of the holy apostles', and that is what his pupil Possidius wrote about his life.[2] Let no one believe that the companion on the path to God was a sinner on account of that rule of which many doubt that he was the author. Let there be one mind among all canons in observing what each of them has vowed and what each finds unharmful to religion in his church.

VI. *Canons who have their houses near the activities of men, such as the canons of St. Quentin in the field and of St. Victor.*[3]

Since we have said a few things above about the canons who live far from men, after dealing with the monks of various habits and orders to the best of our abilities, we must now come to those customs and rules of canons whom we may see as being placed as it were in the middle, being unlike those who withdraw from the

[1] On this interesting passage, and the author's reasons for doubting the authenticity of the rule attributed to St. Augustine, see Dickinson, *Austin Canons*, pp. 63 and 263, who commented that the author 'anticipates modern critics' in his reasoning. On the question of the Augustinian Rule, see Luc Verheijen, *La Règle de saint Augustin* (Paris, 1967).

[2] Possidius, *Vita Augustini*, 5 (*PL*, xxxii. 37); cf. Augustine, *Serm.* 355, 2 (*PL*, xxxix. 1569–70).

[3] The form of this heading in the manuscript (as contrasted to that given by Martène, who put a comma between the 'SanctiQuintinienses' and 'de Prato' and omitted the following 'et') shows that the author was referring to two orders of canons, not three, as I assumed in *Tithes*, pp. 154 and 179, where 'de Prato' was identified as the Augustinian house of St. Stephen at Prato. I have found no other reference to St. Quentin at Beauvais as 'de prato', but it is described in the *Gallia christiana*, ix. 818, as having been founded 'haud longe a moenibus Bellovaci in amaenissimis pratis'.

fugiant, nec sicut illi qui seculares dicuntur, cum hominibus
habitationem suam communicent.¹ Proponuntur enim et isti ad
morum humanorum correctionem, ut mali uidentes eorum uitam
a malicia conuertantur, et conuersiᵃ uel talem uitam aggrediantur,
uel si aggredi non possunt, diligendo, et pro posse imitando et
elemosinas impertiendo pro susceptione iusti, et pro calice aquae
frigidae saltem dato in nomine discipuli, mercedem utriusque
accipiant. Et quoniam illud quod in libro numerorum de tribus
filiis Leui scriptum est, per figuram canonicorum uitae seruire
posse superius memorauimus, et remotos canonicos filiis Caath
assimilauimus, nunc intueamur, si Gerson uel filios eius qui quasi
in medio positi uidentur, tali canonicorum ordini per similitudinem
43 aequiperare ualeamus. Ac primum, quid nomen Gerson innuat,
attendamus. Interpretatur autem Gerson, aduena ibi.² Intende
diligentius, et tali nomine perspecto, si quid congruum uel
officiosum inueneris, studiose notato. Intuere illum qui ait, 'incola
ego sum apud te, et peregrinus sicut omnes patres mei',³ et
intelligere poteris seruos Dei ubicunque sint, 'dum in corpore
sunt peregrinari a Domino',⁴ et ueraciter dici posse apud Deum
esse peregrinos, qui sequuntur ut comprehendant,⁵ et in uia
Dei cum Deo et apud Deum ambulant,⁶ ut ad ipsum peruenire
ualeant. Patres uero suos in hoc imitantur, cum illorum uitam
inspiciendo quam longe a mundi uoluptatibus sese fecerint,
similia operando filios eorum se esse operibus ostendunt. Aduenae
igitur sunt ibi, cum et Deum sibi locum faciunt, et longe se adhuc
a caelesti patria esse cognoscunt.⁷ Si uero melius tibi placet ut
quod dicitur Gerson interpretari aduena ibi referatur ad illud
quod sancti uiri habitant sepius iuxta homines mundanos, et ibi
tanquam aduenae non tanquam indigenae morantur, quia eorum
'conuersatio' non hic, sed 'in caelo est',⁸ habes et in hoc uersum

---

ᵃ et conuersi *add. supra*

company of worldly men entirely and unlike those who are called seculars and who share their living-quarters with other men.[1] They undertake this for the correction of human customs, so that evil men seeing their life should be converted from evil and, being converted, may either enter upon such a life or, if they cannot enter it, in loving it and imitating it as much as they can and in bestowing alms, for the reception of the just, and in giving at the very least a cup of cold water in the name of a disciple, they may accept the reward of both. And since what is written in the book of Numbers about the tribe of the sons of Levi can serve as a figure for the canonical life, as we have noted above, and we have compared the canons living far from men to the sons of Caath, let us now see whether we can compare such an order of canons to Gerson or his sons, who seem to be placed, as it were, in the middle. But first let us see what the name Gerson signifies. Gerson means stranger.[2] Look carefully and, having examined such a name, note carefully whether it contains anything suitable or serviceable. Look at him who says: 'I am a stranger with thee and a sojourner as all my fathers were',[3] and you will be able to understand that God's servants, wherever they are, while 'they are in the body, they are absent from the Lord',[4] and truly it can be said that they are sojourners with God, who follow so that they may obtain[5] and walk in the way of God with God and in the presence of God,[6] so that they may be able to reach Him. Indeed their fathers are imitated in this, when by examining their life, which they have led far from the world's pleasures, by doing similar things they show that they are their sons by their works. Thus they are strangers there, when they make a place for themselves and God and know that they are as yet far from their heavenly home.[7] If it should please you better, let the interpretation of Gerson here as stranger refer to the fact that holy men often live next to men of the world and sojourn there as strangers rather than as natives, since their conversation is not here but in heaven.[8]

---

[1] On the following passage concerning the purpose of canons living near other men, see Dickinson, *Austin Canons*, p. 231, who cited the foundation charter of St. George at Troyes (*c.* 1085) as evidence that these canons aimed to incite others by their good example rather than by their pastoral activity (cf. p. 94 below and intro. pp. xxvi–xxvii on preaching by example rather than by word).

[2] Jerome, *Nom. heb.* (*CC*, lxxii. 75).   [3] Ps. 38: 13.

[4] 2 Cor. 5: 6; cf. Ps.-Jerome, *Brev. in Ps.*, xxxviii, 13 (*PL*, xxvi. 1000B).

[5] 1 Cor. 9: 24.   [6] Baruch 3: 13.

[7] Cf. Ephes. 2: 19.   [8] Phil. 3: 20.

propheticum consonantem, ubi orat, et dicit: 'Incola ego sum in
terra, non abscondas a me mandata tua.'¹ Si uero quod dicitur
aduena ibi referatur de seruo Dei ad ipsum Deum, siue de seruo
Dei ad mundum, utrumque illi seruo Dei congruit, quia et in
hac uita Deum sequitur, nec ut cupit plene consequitur, et ideo
apud Deum peregrinatur, et inter homines tanquam aduena
habitans, 'incolatum suum prolongatum esse et habitationem suam
in Cedar'² heu clamando congeminat. Si autem hanc inter-
pretationem aduenae ad unumquemque fidelem inflectere possumus, quantomagis ad illos, qui hoc non solum uita et moribus
tenent, sed etiam ipso habitu et conuersatione necnon etiam loco,
ut nichil ab eo quod dicitur Gerson id est aduena ibi discrepare
uideantur? Habet ergo haec interpretatio cum canonicis qui in
ciuitatibus uel castellis uel uillis habitant, nec tamen habitationi
hominum sese immiscent aliquam consonantiam, quae et proprie
de illis dicatur, et a caeteris fidelibus non remoueatur. Et quia
de loco et modo habitationis eorum fecimus mentionem, sicut
superius de monachis qui in ciuitatibus uel castellis degunt
diximus, ut officinae eorum habitationem hominum non respiciant,
ita hic canonicis similiter faciendum esse decerno, et istis id est
canonicis rationem illam quae de monachorum habitatione reddita
44 est, custodiendam esse pronuntio. Considerato igitur nomine
Gerson, et interpretatione discussa, intelligi ut credo iam potest,
quod Gersonitarum nomen aᵃ canonicis talibus qui incolatum
mundi actu et loco profitentur, non multum discrepare uideatur.
Iam uero officia Gersonitarum quibus in tabernaculo ministrant
consideremus, si forte canonicis talibus eorum onera uel opera
aptare ualuerimus. Primum ergo inspiciamus, quod a .xxx. annis
et supra usque ad annum .L. id est a perfectione uirtutis usque ad
mortificationem carnis et membrorum 'quae sunt super terram'³
ministrare precipiuntur, et quid postea sequatur intendamus.
Considerandum etiam est, quod sicut Gersonitae pro dignitate
uitae a summo sacerdote uel filio eius Ithamar onera suscipiebant,
ita et isti ab episcopo prout quisque profecerit uel in acolitorum
sorte uel subdiaconorum gradu uel diaconorum dignitate uel

ᵃ a add. supra

You will find confirmation in this verse of the prophet, where he prays and says: 'I am a sojourner on the earth: hide not thy commandments from me.'[1] But whether, as is said, stranger there refers to the servant of God separated from God Himself or to the servant of God separated from the world, either meaning will suit this servant of God, since he follows God in this life and does not follow as fully as he wishes; and so he is a pilgrim on the way to God and lives among men as a stranger, his exile prolonged, and bewails his sojourn in Cedar with groans, crying, 'alas!'[2] If then we can apply this interpretation of stranger to any Christian, can we not all the more to those who follow God not only by life and customs but also by habit and way of living, likewise even in situation, so that nothing seems to disagree here with the meaning of Gerson, that is stranger? Therefore this interpretation has for the canons who live in cities or towns or villages but do not live in other men's houses a certain congruity, which can be appropriately applied to them while not being inapplicable to the rest of Christian men. And since we have mentioned their place and manner of living, just as we have spoken above of monks who live in cities and towns in a way that their workshops do not over-look the houses of men, so I perceive that the canons must act similarly in this respect and declare that the same rule that has been given for the habitation of monks should also be observed 44 by canons. Having considered the name Gerson and discussed its interpretation, we can now, I believe, understand that the name of Gersonites does not seem so unsuitable for such canons who proclaim their exile from the world by their behaviour and place of life. Now we shall consider the duties of the Gersonites by which they minister in the tabernacle and see whether we can equate their burdens and works perhaps to such duties of the canons. First let us see what they are ordered to do from thirty years of age and above to the fiftieth year, that is from the per-fection of virtue to the mortification of the flesh and members, 'which are upon the earth',[3] and then let us examine what comes after. For one must consider that just as the Gersonites received burdens from the high priest or his son Ithamar according to the worthiness of their life, so are they promoted to the condition of acolyte, or the grade of subdeacon, or the dignity of deacon, or the vigilance of priest, according as each one has shown proficiency.

[1] Ps. 118: 19.   [2] Ps. 119: 5.   [3] Col. 3: 5.

sacerdotum uigilantia promouentur. Et ne te turbet quod dicimus, inspice diligentius lectionem numeri, et inuenies alium[a] quasi digniorem ea 'quae ad altare pertinent et uasa ministerii' deferre, 'uelamen iacinctinum' aliumque 'cortinas tabernaculi et tectum faederis' et similia portare, et ut ad minora descendam, alios cortinarum atrii et uelaminis quod 'in introitu' est tabernaculi funiculorumque esse portitores.[1] Et ne putes indifferenter eos ista uel alia portare, subinfertur: 'Et scient singuli, cui debeant oneri mancipari.'[2] Vnde conuenienter conici potest, quod pro uitae merito onerum erat distributio. Similis forma custoditur etiam nunc cum ab episcopo tales canonici ordines sacros prout dignum uidetur quisque sortitur, et gradatim ad sacramenta aecclesiastica promouentur. Si uero te mouet quod istos canonicos Gersonitis assimilamus, uigilanter attende et illorum in lege ritum, et istorum similiter propositum, et intelliges multam esse in utrisque conuenientiam, quam etiam me non piget aliquatenus disserere. Et quia illi sacrorum uasorum et omnium quae ad altare pertinent portitores fuisse memorantur, intueamur quam congruum hoc sit canonicis qui in ciuitatibus et castellis et uillis habitant, ut iuxta homines manentes ad interiora quae significantur et per ea quae ad altare pertinent et per uasa ministerii propter se ipsos resideant, et rursus propter alios ad exteriora respiciant. Intuere etiam sagaciter onera Gersonitarum, licet in illo libro indifferenter ut credo ponantur, quia aliqui eorum ut dixi interiorum ut sunt illa quae ad altare pertinent curam habent, aliqui autem cortinas tabernaculi portantes et tectum federis operimentum aliud non ita in interioribus ut priores morantur, illi scilicet qui uasa ministerii et ea quae ad altare pertinent ferunt. Nec illi ergo Gersonitae relinquantur, qui paene expositi et interiora paene relinquentes, tentorium quod pendet in introitu faederis tabernaculi cortinas atrii et uelamen in introitu[b] quod est ante tabernaculum portare memorantur. In hac trina diuisione Gersonitae partiti, possunt significare canonicos qui in aecclesiis quae iuxta

---

[a] alium *add. supra*　　　[b] in introitu *add. supra*

And in case you should be disturbed by what we say, study very carefully the lesson in Numbers and you will find that one man, more worthy as it were, carries those things that pertain to the altar, 'the vessels of the ministry, the violet covering, and another carries the curtains of the tabernacle, the roof of the covenant, and the like, and, to descend to lesser things, others are carriers of the curtains of the courtyard and the hanging in the entry of the tabernacle and the cords'.[1] And in case you consider it immaterial whether they carry the one or the other, there is added: 'And each man shall know to what burden he must be assigned.'[2] And so one may suitably conjecture that there was a distribution of burdens according to the merits of their life. A similar method is adopted nowadays when such canons are granted holy orders by the bishop, to each as seems worthy, and gradually they are promoted to the sacraments of the church. Should it disturb you that we liken these canons to the Gersonites, examine carefully both the observance of the former in the law and the calling of the latter, and you will understand that many elements of both are comparable, and I find it not unpleasing to discuss them a little. And remembering those who were carriers of the holy vessels and everything pertaining to the altar, let us understand how fitting this is for the canons who live in cities and towns or villages, in order that, living next to men, for their own sake they stay in attendance on internal things, which are signified by the altar's accoutrements and by the vessels of the ministry, and for the sake of others they may look towards exterior things. Examine wisely the burdens of the Gersonites, although I believe that they are enumerated in that book without distinction, since some of them, as I have said, look after interior things, such as those which pertain to the altar, and others, carrying the curtains of the tabernacle and the roof of the covenant and the other covering, do not stay inside like the first ones, that is those who carry the vessels of the ministry and the things that pertain to the altar. Nor should those Gersonites be left aside, therefore, who, virtually in the open, virtually abandoning interior concerns, are noted as carrying the hanging that hangs in the entry of the tabernacle of the covenant, the curtains of the courtyard, and the covering in the entrance which is before the tabernacle. The Gersonites arranged in this threefold division can stand for the canons who lead their life by

---

[1] Num. 4: 25–6.   [2] Num. 4: 27.

homines sunt professionem seruiendi Deo faciunt, quorum
quidam ab episcopis ordinati ad communes ordines aecclesiae
sub manu abbatis sui quasi 'sub manu Ithamar filii summi
sacerdotis uiuunt[a]',[1] et prouida dispensatione prout ipse abbas
unumquemque ualere nouit, unum introrsum quasi circa altare
et circa uasa ministerii manere precipit, alium uero nec totum
interius nec totum exterius quasi ad cortinas et ad tectum faederis
quae quidem ut credo in loco interiorum erant, sed de longe uideri[b]
poterant pro merito uitae deputat, alium autem quem in exterioribus ualere conspicit, quasi ad tentorium 'quod pendet in introitu
faederis tabernaculi' et ad 'cortinas atrii'[2] fidenter relaxat. Et ut
manifestius fiat quod dicimus, unus in claustro retinetur, ut in
interioribus Deo seruiat, alius in eodem loco curas fratrum suorum
et hospitum uel peregrinorum suscipit, alius equidem ad obaedien-
46 tiam longe et ad parroechiam dirigitur. Et quia de parroechiis quas
ipsi suscipiunt susceptasque regunt fecimus mentionem, dignum
est ut de hoc pauca dicamus. Nam audiui plerosque sacerdotes
uel clericos laudantes quidem ordinem talium canonicorum,
sed murmurantes quod qui seculum reliquerunt, rursus ad seculi
homines curandos remittantur, quasi dignum non sit, eos secularia negotia uel propter se uel propter alios tractare. Quapropter
illud primum intuendum est, quod eadem familia Gersonitarum
cortinas atrii in ministerium suscipit. Atrium itaque extra tabernaculum erat, et prope tabernaculum. Nam et atria domus extra
domum sunt et iuxta domum, domuique inherent, ut nullus de
domo egredi possit uel ingredi, nisi per atrium quod domui
iungitur. Et attende quod illi qui cortinas atrii ferebant, illorum
uitam qui subtiliter ad aecclesiam uenientes inuestigant, significare possunt. Illud etiam inspice, quod haec familia cum uasis
altaris cum funiculis et uasis ministerii non nisi cortinas et tectum
siue uelamina uel tentoria et cortinas itidem atrii[c] portare memorantur, quae omnia subtilia fuisse si exodum legeris inuenies.[3] Et
quia similitudinem de hac familia ad canonicos qui iuxta homines
sunt trahere uolumus, primum intueamur officium familiae illius

---

serving God in churches next to men, of whom some, ordained
by the bishop to the common orders of the church, live under the
control of their abbot, as if 'under the hand of Ithamar, the son of
the high priest',[1] and by a provident dispensation, as the abbot
himself considers suitable in each case, he orders one to stay inside,
as it were near the altar and the vessels of the ministry; he deputes
another, depending upon the merits of his life, to stay not entirely
inside and not entirely outside, as it were near the curtains and the
roof of the covenant, which I believe were in an interior place
but could be seen from a distance; and he confidently assigns yet
another, whom he considers suitable for the outside, to be by the
hanging 'that hangeth in the entry of the tabernacle of the covenant'
and by the curtains of the courtyard.[2] And to make clearer what
we have said: one is kept in the cloister so that he may serve
God in internal things; another undertakes in the same place the
care of his brothers, of guests, and of pilgrims; and another is
sent out far away to a dependency and to a parish. And since we
have mentioned the parishes which they take on and having taken
on direct, it is fitting that we should say a little about them. For
I have heard many priests and clerics praising such an order
of canons but complaining that those who have left the world are
sent back again to take care of men in the world, as if secular
affairs, either on account of themselves or of others, were not
proper for them. And because of this one must first examine the
undertaking by the same family of the Gersonites of the duty
of the curtains of the courtyard. The courtyard was outside the
tabernacle but next to it. And the courtyards of a house are outside
the house and next to it and are thus an integral part of the house,
so that no one can leave the house or enter it unless they go through
the adjoining courtyard. And you can see that those who carried
the curtains of the courtyard can signify by their life those who
scrupulously investigate those coming to church. See this also,
that this family was said to carry with the vessels of the altar and
with the cords and the vessels of the ministry only the curtains
and the roof, or covering, and in the same manner the hanging
and curtains of the courtyard, which you will find, if you read
Exodus,[3] were all delicate objects. And since we wish to discuss
the likeness of this family to the canons who live next to men, let
us see how clean the duties of this family were and how demanding

---

[1] Num. 7: 8.　　　[2] Num. 4: 25–6.　　　[3] Exod. 26–7.

quam mundum fuerit et quam subtile. Quid mundius poterat
inueniri cortinis tabernaculi cum factae sunt, quid subtilius?
Forsitan omnium seruorum Dei mundiciam praefigurabant, et
subtilitatem siue in scripturis intelligendis indicant,[a] siue in
moribus cohercendis uel suis uel aliorum, ne ab irruente iniquitate
tanquam interiora tabernaculi a tempestate ledantur. Si igitur
omnia haec mundiciam et subtilitatem seruorum Dei indicant,
quantomagis illorum qui hoc et opere exercent, et habitu uel
habitatione testantur? Si enim tales canonicos prudenter inspicias, et eorum professionem consideres, inuenies eos qui ex his
intus in claustro resident actus suos sociorumque subtiliter
inuestigare, ne quid sit quod oculos diuinae maiestatis offendat,
eos etiam qui exterius uel propter obaedientiam uel parroechiam
mittuntur subtiliter uel suos actus uel sibi commissorum pensare,
et super omnia circa ministerium altaris mundiciam tenere. Si
igitur ut premissum est illi leuitae qui cortinas atrii ferebant eos
canonicos prefigurare possunt qui exteriorum hominum facta
subtiliter pensant, iam non erit absurdum si canonici ipsi populos
regant, qui eorum facta discutere, et sui officii respectu munda
47 facere nouerunt. Si autem requiratur quare et ipsi seruos habeant
et ancillas, et cur sicut iudices seculares eos regant et protegant,
superius de monachis haec eadem agentibus ratio reddita sequi
debet. De decimis uero quas suscipiunt, nulla questio esse
debet, quia ut leuitae et sacerdotes quod suum est requirunt.
Addimus etiam predictae rationi, quod leuitis precipiente Domino
'urbes ad habitandum' datae sunt,[1] et 'oppida sex in fugitiuorum
auxilia, et alia oppida .XL.VIII. cum suburbanis suis'.[2] Ex quibus
omnibus liquet, quod quidam leuitarum in tabernaculo et circa
tabernaculum uersabantur, quidam uero longe positi populos
remotos docebant quae Dei sunt, obaedientes summo pontifici
et filiis eius. Similem ergo formam canonici iuxta homines positi
custodiunt, quosdam in matrice aecclesia tanquam in tabernaculo
retinentes, quosdam uero longe ad docendos et regendos populos
dirigentes, ut de redditibus et decimis fidelium et ipsi uiuant, et

---

[a] indicant *add. in marg.*

of delicacy. What could be found more clean than the curtains of the tabernacle, when they have been made, and what more exquisite? Perhaps they prefigured the cleanliness of all the servants of God and indicate their scrupulousness either in understanding the scriptures or in restraining the behaviour of themselves or others, lest they should be damaged by a flood of iniquity, as the interior of the temple would be by a tempest. If therefore all these things indicate the cleanliness and meticulousness of God's servants, how much more do they show concerning them who practise them by their work and bear witness to them by their way of life and place of living? For if you examine such canons prudently and consider their calling, you will find that those of them who live in the cloister for these reasons meticulously investigate their own and their companions' actions, lest there should be anything to offend the eye of divine majesty; those also who are sent outside on account either of a dependency or a parish ponder their own actions and those of the people committed to them scrupulously, and above all else they maintain cleanliness in what concerns the service of the altar. If therefore, as I have assumed, those levites who carried the curtains of the courtyard can prefigure the canons who ponder the deeds of men outside scrupulously, it would not be absurd if these canons should direct the people, since they know how to discuss their deeds and, by virtue of their office, how to make them clean. If it is asked why they also have serfs and bondswomen and why they should govern and protect them like worldly judges, the reason I gave above why certain monks do the same must be my answer. There should be no question about the tithes they take, since like the levites and the priests they ask for what is theirs. And we add to the reason already given that 'cities to dwell in'[1] were given to the levites at God's command and six cities 'for refuge to fugitives' and another 'forty-eight with their suburbs'.[2] From all this it is clear that certain of the levites remained in the tabernacle and near by and that others were at a distance teaching distant people the things of God, in obedience to the high priest and his sons. Therefore a similar order is observed by the canons who are sent among men, some being retained in the mother church, as if in the tabernacle, others being sent away to teach and govern the people, so that they may live from the rents and tithes of the faithful, and may

[1] Num. 35: 3.   [2] Num. 35: 6–7.

quod superfuerit, fratribus suis ad aecclesiam tanquam ad tabernaculum sacerdotibus ac ministris deferant.[1] Si uero requiras
quare ipsi Gersonitae id est aduenae ibi sub manu Ithamar filii
summi sacerdotis qui interpretatur amaritudo[2] constituantur, fa-
cilis patet responsio, quia qui aduenas se in hoc seculo nouerunt
'dum sunt in corpore a Domino peregrinantes',[3] salutifera et a
Deo data amaritudine patriam semper requirunt, et sic sub filio
summi sacerdotis Ithamar id est sub dilato desiderio patriae
caelestis adipiscendae sub quadam amaritudine uiuunt, Deoque
48 ministrant. Ecce dum in 'umbra futurorum bonorum'[4] id est in
ueteri lege canonicos uel leuitas sacerdotesque istius temporis
adumbratos fuisse querimus, et post illam umbram ueritatem
sequimur, ille noster Iesus nobis ad memoriam reuocatur, qui
non umbratice sed ueraciter de humana infirmitate natus, et
iuste uel regulariter inter homines uiuens, et ideo merito quasi
leuites assumptus, 'sacerdos' uel pontifex factus 'est in aeternum
secundum ordinem Melchisedech'.[5] Inquiramus ergo de illo, si
forte aliquid egerit, unde tales canonicos representauerit. Lege
illum diligenter in euangelio secundum Lucam proximum
passioni, euntem secundum consuetudinem in montem Oliuarum.
Sequuti sunt autem eum et discipuli. Et cum peruenisset ad locum,
dixit illis: 'Orate, ne intretis in temptationem. At ipse auulsus
est ab eis, quantum iactus est lapidis. Et positis genibus orabat
dicens: Pater si uis, transfer calicem istum a me. Verumtamen,
non mea uoluntas, sed tua fiat. Apparuit autem illi angelus de
caelo, confortans eum. Et factus in agonia, prolixius orabat. Et
factus est sudor eius sicut guttae sanguinis decurrentis in terram.
Et cum surrexisset ab oratione, et uenisset ad discipulos, inuenit
eos dormientes prae tristicia. Et ait illis: Surgite orate, ne intretis
in temptationem.'[6] Intueamur pontificem nostrum dominum
Iesum qui penetrauit caelos, egressum secundum consuetudinem
in montem Oliuarum, ut omnibus se sequentibus suam misericordiam insinuaret.[a] Egrediatur et canonicus de turbine huius
uitae cum Domino, ut omnium misereatur, et sit 'omnibus[b]

---

[a] insunuaret *MS*.   [b] omnibus *add. supra*

bring back what is left over to their brothers in the church, as to the priests and ministers in the tabernacle.[1] If you ask why these Gersonites, that is strangers, were placed under the command of Ithamar, the son of the high priest, whose name means bitterness,[2] the answer is easy, since those who know themselves to be strangers in this world, 'while they are in the body they are absent from the Lord',[3] always seek a country, by means of a salubrious bitterness given by God, and thus serve God under the command of the son of the high priest Ithamar, that is, in a deferred desire to reach their heavenly home, they live in a certain bitterness and they minister 48 to God. Behold, while we are seeking in 'a shadow of the good things to come',[4] that is in the old law, that the levites and the priests of that time adumbrated the canons, and while we are seeking the truth after that shadow, our Jesus is recalled to our memory, who born not in shadow but truly from human weakness and living justly and by a rule among men, and so deservedly taken up like the levites, was made 'priest' and pontiff 'for ever according to the order of Melchisedech'.[5] Let us inquire about Him to see whether He perhaps did anything to represent such an order of canons. Read carefully in the gospel of St. Luke where when He was near His passion, going according to His custom to the Mount of Olives, His disciples also followed Him and when He was come to the place He said to them: 'Pray lest ye enter into temptation.' And he was withdrawn away from them a stone's cast. And kneeling down he prayed, saying: 'Father, if thou wilt, remove this chalice from me: but yet not my will, but thine be done.' And there appeared to him an angel from heaven, strengthening him. And being in agony he prayed the longer. And his sweat became as drops of blood, trickling down upon the ground. And when he rose up from prayer and was coming to the disciples, he found them sleeping for sorrow. And he said to them: 'Arise: pray, lest you enter into temptation.'[6] See our priest the Lord Jesus, who entered into heaven, who went out according to His custom into the Mount of Olives, so that His mercy would be made known to all who followed Him. The canon also goes out with the Lord from the tumult of this life, to show mercy to

---

[1] On the reception of tithes and parochial revenues by these canons who performed pastoral work, see Constable, *Tithes*, p. 179 and *passim*.

[2] Jerome, *Nom. heb.* (*CC*, lxxii. 76).

[3] 2 Cor. 5: 6.

[4] Heb. 10: 1.

[5] Ps. 109: 4; Heb. 5: 6.

[6] Luke 22: 40–6.

omnia', ut omnes lucrifaciat.[1] Et nota, quod secundum consuetudinem in montem Oliuarum egredi dicitur. Quis enim melius secundum consuetudinem in montem Oliuarum egredi iure dicatur, quam ille 'pater misericordiarum',[2] qui est etiam mons montium, in quo placet Deo habitare usque in finem? Sic et canonicus debet facere, imitando illum qui tulit omnium uulnera, ut omnibus misereretur. Sequuti sunt autem illum et discipuli, uolentes ire quo ille ibat, et non ualentes, sicut Petro predixerat.[3] Infirmi enim adhuc erant. Hoc et nobis sepe contingit cum bona coram hominibus facimus ut 'imitatores nostri sint, sicut et nos Christi'.[4] Sequuntur autem nos sicut illi discipuli adhuc infirmi sequebantur Dominum, sed in omnibus nos sequi non possunt. Cum enim perueniunt nobiscum ad locum orationis sicut illi discipuli cum Domino, et inuitantur a nobis ad orationem ne intrent in temptationem,[5] non possunt diu orare, non possunt diu nobiscum stare. Quid igitur nobis faciendum est? Auellamur ab eis cum Domino quantum iactus est lapidis, id est ad perfectionem feramur, quantum homo lapidem Christum imitari potest, relinquentes ad tempus populorum imbecillitatem, et pro eis orantes, ut Christi passionibus nobiscum ualeant communicare.[6] 'Positisque genibus orabat dicens: Pater si uis, transfer calicem istum a me. Verumtamen non mea uoluntas, sed tua fiat.'[7] Manifestum est omnibus haec dicere Dominum, non propter se qui 'potestatem habuit ponendi' animam suam 'et iterum sumendi eam',[8] sed propter illos 'qui in hoc tabernaculo ingemiscentes nollent expoliari sed superuestiri, ut absorbeatur mortale a uita'.[9] Quid igitur? Istam orationem quam filius optulit patri, nullus iam fidelium et precipue canonicorum uel quorumlibet Dei seruorum dicere potest? Potest ut credo. Licet enim in Dei seruitio magis exercitato infirmioris personam in se suscipere, sicut et Dominus clamat caput pro membris, nec est absurdum si maius membrum clamet pro minore, sicut non est absurdum maiorem digitum minorem tegere uel defendere. Dicat ergo perfectus quilibet, dicat et canonicus, qui cum infirmo infirmatur, cum scandalizato uritur, et oret suscipiens in se personam alterius:

all men, to be 'all things to all men', to win over all men.[1] And note
that He is said to have gone into the Mount of Olives according to
His custom. Who can be said to have gone with greater justice
into the Mount of Olives than that Father of mercies,[2] who is the
mount of mountains, in whom it pleases God to live to the very end?
So should the canon live, imitating Him who bore all men's wounds
so that He might have mercy on all. His disciples also followed
Him wishing to go where He went and not being able to as He
had foretold to Peter.[3] For as yet they were weak. This also often
happens to us, when we do good in the sight of men, so that they
may be 'followers of us as we also are of Christ'.[4] They follow us
just as the disciples, still weak, followed the Lord, but they cannot
follow us in everything. For when they have reached with us the
place of prayer, as the disciples had with the Lord, and are asked
by us to pray that they enter not into temptation,[5] they cannot
pray for long and cannot stand with us for long. What then must
we do? Let us withdraw a stone's cast from them with the Lord,
that is let us be carried to perfection as far as a man can imitate
Christ the stone, leaving the weakness of the people for a time
and praying for them so that they may be able to partake with
us of the sufferings of Christ.[6] 'And kneeling down he prayed,
saying: Father, if thou wilt, remove this chalice from me; but yet
not my will, but thine be done.'[7] It is clear to all that the Lord
said these things not for Himself, who had 'the power to lay down
his life and take it up again',[8] but for those who groaning in this
tabernacle 'would not be unclothed, but clothed upon, that that
which is mortal may be swallowed up by life'.[9] What then?
Can none of the faithful, and especially the canons or any whatever
of God's servants speak that prayer which the Son offered to the
Father? I believe that they can. For although God's service requires great labour for the weaker to take up a person into himself,
as the Lord cries out, the head for the members, it is not absurd
if the greater member should cry out for the lesser, just as it is
not absurd for the greater finger to protect and defend the lesser.
Let whoever is perfect say, therefore, and let also the canon, who
suffers weakness with the weak and distress with the fallen, say
and pray, taking up in himself the person of another: 'Father, if it

---

[1] 1 Cor. 9: 22. [2] 2 Cor. 1: 3. [3] Cf. Matt. 26: 41.
[4] 1 Cor. 4: 16; 11: 1. [5] Matt. 26: 41, etc. [6] 1 Pet. 4: 13.
[7] Luke 22: 41–2. [8] John 10: 18. [9] 2 Cor. 5: 4.

'Pater, si fieri potest, transeat a me calix iste.'[1] Video enim fratres
meos uiscera mea multum trepidantes relinquere usum pristinum,
et precor ut a uisceribus meis transeat calix[a] iste inueteratae
consuetudinis, relinquantque mundum qui transit cum concupiscentiis suis,[2] et relinquant et transeat ab eis calix 'qui mixtus est
mero in calice irae Dei',[3] recedatque ab eis moriaturque in eis
calix Babylonis[4] id est cupiditas secularis, ut possint et ipsi suscipere calicem salutarem, et nomen Domini perfecte inuocare.[5]
Quod si fieri non potest quod uolumus 'omnes homines esse sicut'
nos ipsos,[6] 'non nostra uoluntas sed tua fiat',[7] qui cuius uis
misereris 'et quem' uis obduras,[8] et perfectos 'id ipsum sapere'
facis,[9] et 'imperfectum' nostrum 'uiderunt oculi tui'.[10] Non enim
qui adhuc perfecti non sunt omnino peribunt, sed credentes salui
fient.[11] Haec dicens canonicus, qui forte ex precepto abbatis sui
regit plebem Dei, uel qui interius manens pro plebe Dei orationem
fundit, perfecte potest dicere ut credo illam dominicam uocem,
fratris sui infirmitatem suam esse deputans. Si autem et hoc
communiter dicat, et pro se et pro aliis, uidebitur, orare, ut
'passiones peccatorum quae operantur in membris nostris ut
fructum ferant morti',[12] transeant a nobis, ut 'liberati a peccato'[13]
tanquam a calice mortis, 'uota nostra reddamus in atriis domus
Domini, in medio Ierusalem'.[14] Quid autem dicemus de tali
canonico uel leuita? Numquid ipse quem inuocat et cui 'optem-
perat pater spirituum'[15] relinquit eum inconsolatum? Non. Vide
ergo quis effectus illam dominicam orationem sequatur: 'Apparuit
autem illi angelus de caelo, confortans eum.'[16] Apparet etiam nobis
nunc 'magni consilii angelus',[17] 'panis ille qui de caelo descendit',[18]
ut cor hominis confortaret, cum pro nobis et pro eius populo
supplicamus, effectum orationibus nostris prebendo, et ut 'sine

---

[a] calix *add. supra*

can be done, let this chalice pass from me.'[1] For I see my brothers, my bowels, fearing greatly to give up the old ways, and I pray that this chalice of ingrained custom should pass from my bowels and that they should leave the world which passes away with its concupiscences,[2] and that the chalice 'which is mingled with pure wine in the cup of God's wrath'[3] should leave them, should pass from them, and that the chalice of Babylon,[4] that is worldly desire, should die in them, so that they may be able to take up the chalice of salvation and call upon the name of the Lord perfectly.[5] And if what we desire cannot be done, 'that all men were even as ourselves',[6] let 'not our will but thine be done',[7] thou who 'hast mercy on whom thou wilt and hardenest whom thou wilt',[8] and who makest the perfect 'to be of one mind',[9] and 'thy eyes did see our imperfect being'.[10] For those who are not yet perfect shall not perish entirely, but they that believe shall be saved.[11] Saying this, the canon who perhaps rules God's people by order of his abbot or he who stays within and pours forth prayer for God's people can, I believe, say perfectly those words of the Lord taking on Himself His brother's weakness. If he should also say this publicly, he will be seen to pray both for himself and for others, so that 'the passions of sins which did work in our members to bring forth fruit unto death'[12] may pass away from us, and that 'being freed from sin',[13] as from the chalice of death, 'we shall pay our vows in the courts of the house of the Lord, in the midst of Jerusalem'.[14] What shall we say of such a canon or levite? Will He whom he invokes and whom the father of spirits obeys[15] leave him unconsoled? No. See what effect proceeds from that prayer of the Lord: 'And there appeared to him an angel from heaven strengthening him.'[16] There will also appear now to us 'the angel of great counsel',[17] 'that bread which cometh down from heaven',[18] and will strengthen the heart of man when we pray for ourselves and his people, giving effect to our prayers and comforting us so that we may

[1] Luke 22: 42.
[2] 1 John 2: 17.
[3] Apoc. 14: 10.
[4] Jer. 51: 7.
[5] Gen. 4: 26, etc.
[6] 1 Cor. 7: 7.
[7] Luke 22: 42.
[8] Rom. 9: 18.
[9] Rom. 15: 5.
[10] Ps. 138: 16.
[11] 1 Cor. 1: 21.
[12] Rom. 7: 5.
[13] Rom. 6: 18.
[14] Ps. 115: 18–19.
[15] Heb. 12: 9.
[16] Luke 22: 43.
[17] Introit (from Isa. 9: 6) to 3rd mass of Christmas, and other liturgical uses listed by Karl Marbach, *Carmina scripturarum* (Strasburg, 1907 [reprint Hildesheim, 1963]), pp. 306–7.
[18] John 6: 33.

intermissione oremus'[1] confortando, et ne quid in oratione deesset,
50 quod in capite Christo Iesu non precederet, uide ipsum in oratione
laborantem, unde etiam sequitur: 'Et factus in agonia prolixius
orabat.'[2] Quid igitur est quod dominus meus Iesus orans patrem
in agonia fit, nisi hoc, quod nos cum oramus, et ipso cum effectu
nostrae orationi prestito apparente nosque confortante, aura illa
secularis cogitationis uel carnalis infirmitatis seu fauor humanae
laudis exagitare cupit, et ab oratione diuellere? Quapropter agon
ille quem assumpsit Iesus arripiendus est, licet alio modo, ut
refugiamus illa secularia et carnalia, et prolixius orantes, turbines
51 cogitationum fluitantium superemus. Sequitur: 'Et factus est
sudor eius, sicut guttae sanguinis decurrentis in terram.'[3] Primum
inspice dominum Iesum in agonia prolixius orantem, sudore suo
laborem orationis commendantem, deinde intuere ipsum sudorem
ad instar sanguinis fluentem in terra, ut labor orationis eius laboris
nostri esset initium, et sudor eius testimonii nostri quod pro Iesu
testificamur, et ad terram hoc est ad terrenos homines uelut passio
quaedam decurrit fieret incitamentum. Si enim inspicias uigilantes
nos et orantes quomodo stupeant homines et dicant supra se esse
quod agimus, intelliges laborem nostrum pro testimonio Iesu
uelut sanguinem id est passionem fluxisse et peruenisse ad terram
cum homines orationes et uigilias nostras magnam esse iudicent
52 passionem. Et uide quid sequatur sudorem illum sanguineum: 'Et
cum surrexisset ab oratione, et uenisset ad discipulos, inuenit eos
dormientes pre tristicia.'[4] Quid autem est quod cum Iesus orat,
discipuli contristati dormiunt, nisi quod nobis orantibus et in
orando laborantibus, homines illi adhuc infirmi et ad imitationem
nostri assurgere adhuc non ualentes, sopiuntur tamen iam a
uoluntate carnali? Tristicia autem quae eos sequitur et dormire
facit, quid est aliud quam paenitentia peccatorum, quae mentem
terret, et a peccato dormire facit? Quae cum superno respectu
contingit, tunc ueniendum est cum Iesu ad discipulos, hoc est ad
homines adhuc infirmos, tunc increpandi, tunc admonendi, tunc
excitandi, tunc dicendum est eis, quod in sequentibus dicit
Iesus: 'Quid dormitis?'[5] Plus[6] uos oportet facere, quam mala et

'pray without ceasing',[1] and so that nothing should be lacking in our prayer that does not come before in our head, Jesus Christ. 50 See Him labouring in prayer, and after that follows 'and being in agony he prayed the longer'.[2] What then does it mean for my Lord Jesus praying to the Father to be in agony, except that when we pray, and when He appears as the result of our prayer and comforts us, that gust of worldly thought or of carnal weakness or the applause of human praise seeks to disturb us and distract us from prayer? And because of this that agony which Jesus bore must be seized on, though in another way, so that we may take refuge from the secular and the carnal and, praying the longer, 51 we shall overcome the whirlwinds of distracting thoughts. There follows: 'And his sweat became as drops of blood, trickling down upon the ground.'[3] First see the Lord Jesus praying the longer in His agony, commending the labour of prayer by His sweat; next see the sweat itself flowing on the ground like blood, so that the labour of His prayer should be the beginning of our labour and His sweat should inspire the testimony which we bear for Jesus, and which flows to the ground, that is to earthly men, like a kind of passion. For if you look at us watching and praying, and see how men are amazed, and say that what we do is far above them, you will understand that our labour in testimony of Jesus has flowed down and reached the ground like blood, that is the passion, since men consider our prayers and vigils to be a great 52 passion. And see what follows that bloody sweat: 'And when he rose up from prayer and was come to the disciples he found them sleeping for sorrow.'[4] What does it mean that while Jesus prays His saddened disciples sleep except that to us praying and labouring in prayer those men who are still weak and not yet strong enough to rise up to imitate us are at least already at rest from carnal desire? What else is the sadness which pursues them and drives them to sleep but the penitence of sinners which alarms the mind and makes it quiescent from sin? When this penitence touches upon heavenly concerns, then we should come with Jesus to the apostles, that is to men still weak; then they should be reproved, admonished, encouraged; then we should say to them as Jesus said in the following verse: 'Why sleep you?'[5] You[6]

---

[1] 1 Thess. 5: 17.   [2] Luke 22: 43.   [3] Luke 22: 44.   [4] Luke 22: 45.
[5] Luke 22: 46.   [6] There begins at this point an apostrophe going to 'a via Dei deuiabitis' ('from God's way').

cupiditates mundi relinquere. Salubris est quidem somnus iste,
'quiescere' scilicet secundum Ysaiam 'agere peruerse',[1] sed uidete
quod dictum est, 'declina a malo et fac bonum',[2] et illud quod
sequitur in eodem propheta, 'discite bene facere'.[3] 'Surgite' ergo
'et orate ne intretis in temptationem.'[4] Si enim tepidi fueritis,
dominus Iesus 'euomens uos ex ore suo'[5] patietur uos 'induci in
temptationem',[6] quam ferre non poteritis, sicque a uia Dei deuiabitis. Ecce illa quae fecit Iesus uerus leuita uerusque sacerdos,
propinquans passioni et orans diutius, canonicis qui iuxta homines
sunt bene ut credo aptari possunt, quae canonicus obseruans
recte regularis poterit appellari, et si regimen super homines
seculares habuerit, et ad bona eos prouocauerit, non poterit ab
aliquo proinde iudicari. Sed dum meum Iesum qui fons est et
origo totius boni istorum etiam canonicorum opera suscepisse
conitio, mens reminiscitur illorum, qui in primitiua aecclesia
Ierosolimis morabantur, quos sancti apostoli corporaliter propter
predicationem euangelii relinquentes, mente quidem cum eis
morabantur, et tempore famis 'quae facta est sub Claudio' de
elemosinis credentium ut in actibus eorum legitur sustentare
satagebant.[7] Quae si recte inspicias, uidebis canonicos qui iuxta
homines sunt similia agere, cum et illi qui interius quasi qui in
Ierosolimis morantur illos qui exterius uel propter predicationem
et regimen uel propter obaedientiam sunt orationibus suis comi-
tantur, illi uero qui exterius quasi apostoli per mundum sunt
interius Deo seruientes magnificant, et ne causam progrediendi
et minus orandi habeant, de elemosinis fidelium reficere non
desinunt. Sed et illud attende, quod Gersonitis de quibus paulo
antea loquebamur plaustra et boues dati sunt, ut illorum infirmitas
releuaretur, ne sub onere suo deficerent. Quid enim sunt uehicula,
nisi infirmitatis nostrae remedia? Habemus ergo plaustra, habemus
et boues, quibus onera quae in domo Domini suscipimus ferun-
tur, cum perfecte orationi studentes, plaustrum nostrum id est
uolubilitatem et mortalitatem nostram, per boues id est, per

must do more than renounce the evils and lusts of the world. That sleep is indeed salutary, that is, according to Isaiah, to 'cease to act perversely',[1] but see what is written: 'Decline from evil and do good',[2] and what follows in the same prophet: 'Learn to do well',[3] 'Arise' therefore and 'pray, lest you enter into temptation.'[4] For if you are lukewarm, the Lord Jesus 'vomiting you out of His mouth',[5] will let you be led into temptation,[6] which you will not be able to bear, and you will thus turn aside from God's way. Behold those things which Jesus, the true levite and true priest, did when he was near the time of His passion and long in prayer, can well be applied to the canons who live near to men, I believe; a canon observing them properly can be called a regular, and if he has the governance of worldly men and calls them to good things, he will not be liable to judgement for it by anyone. But while I conjecture that my Jesus, who is the source and origin of all good, took up the works of the canons, I am put in mind of those who stayed in the primitive church of Jerusalem, with whom the holy apostles, while leaving them bodily because of the need to preach the gospel, remained in their minds, and at a time of famine 'which came to pass in the time of Claudius' were able to sustain themselves sufficiently on the alms of the faithful, as is described in Acts.[7] And if you look at it properly you will see that the canons who live near men act in the same way, when those who stay within like those in Jerusalem commit to their prayers those who are without either for the sake of preaching and pastoral care or to perform a duty. But those who are outside are like the apostles in the world and glorify those serving God within, and lest these should have reason to go out and pray less, they never cease to receive the alms of the faithful. But remember that the Gersonites, whom we have spoken of a little earlier, were given wagons and oxen, so that their weakness might be helped and they should not become disheartened under their burden. For what are vehicles but a remedy for weakness? Therefore we have wagons and oxen to bear the burdens we receive in the Lord's house, when, zealous for perfect prayer, we draw our wagon around, that is our mutability and mortality, by oxen, that is by

53

[1] Isa. 1: 16.
[2] Ps. 36: 27.
[3] Isa. 1: 17.
[4] Luke 22: 46.
[5] Apoc. 3: 16.
[6] Matt. 6: 13.
[7] Acts 11: 28–30.

predicatores uel operarios exteriores cum oneribus nostris id est
cum laboribus seruiendi Deo circumducimus. Per illos enim qui
nobis in exterioribus rebus ministrant oratio nostra multum
iuuatur, quia uix fieri potest, ut perfecte quis orationi studeat, qui
mentem uel exterioribus rebus uel laboribus corporalibus occupat.
Quod si quis etiam hoc agere preualet, quia in aecclesia tam perfecti
uiri non desunt, cum apostolo laudet Deum, qui manibus laborabat
ne quem grauaret,[1] et fratrum memoriam semper in orationibus
habebat, sicut ipse de Romanis se agere perhibet.[2] Vtuntur autem
isti potestate sibi concessa, habentes licentiam ut 'qui euangelium
annuntiant, de euangelio uiuant',[3] scientes non esse magnum,
quandoquidem ipsi 'spiritualia seminant', si populorum 'carnalia
55 metant'.[4] Si autem quis michi obiciat, quod multi in his sunt
qui euangelium annuntiare nesciunt, sicut sunt simplices quique
uel conuersi, de hoc respondeo, quia qui bene uiuit, et propositum bene uiuendi habet, professionemque suam quantum potest
sequitur, de hoc recte dicitur quod euangelizat, id est bona
annuntiat. Melius enim michi annuntiare uidetur qui bene uiuit,
quam qui bene loquitur. Ille enim pro bono opere uel bono odore
accipiet remunerationem, hic autem quia sciuit 'uoluntatem
Domini sui et fecit' digna plagis, 'uapulans multis' accipiet
56 dampnationem.[5] Quod si aliquem mouet quod plerique canonici,
ex his dico qui iuxta homines mundanos habitant manibus non
laborant, primum possumus breuiter respondere, quod dicit
apostolus: 'Corporalis exercitatio ad modicum utilis est, pietas
autem ad omnia utilis.'[6] Quod enim dicit ad modicum esse utilem
corporalem exercitationem, ostendit quidem illam aliquantulum
ualere, sed non adeo ut super hoc preceptum alicui imponat,
uel si non laboret corporaliter, deteriorem iudicet. 'Pietas autem'
quam 'ad omnia utilem' esse denuntiat, in canonicis qui iuxta
homines morantur, a magistris tunc maxima exhibetur, cum in
claustris retinentur, ne progredientes mundana iuxta se posita
uideant, quibus uisis in illis hereant, et infirmas mentes molliant,
et tali uisu dispereant. Nam laus claustralium esse solet, si diu
in claustro fuerint, si mundana uidere contempserint. Si autem

preachers and exterior workers, with our burdens, that is our labours in serving God. Our prayer is much helped by those who minister to us in external things, for it can hardly be offered if he who wishes to become perfect in prayer has also to occupy his mind with external matters and corporeal labours. And if anyone excels in doing this, for such perfect men are not lacking in the church, let him praise God with the apostle, who worked with his hands lest he should be a burden to anyone[1] and kept the memory of his brothers always in his prayers just as he said he kept the Romans.[2] They make use of that power granted to them, with the liberty that those who proclaim the gospel may live from the gospel,[3] knowing it is not a great thing, seeing that they 'sow spiritual things' if they 'reap carnal things' from the people.[4]

5 If anyone should object that there are many among them who do not know how to proclaim the gospel, as for example the unlearned ones or the *conversi*, I reply that whoever lives well and has the intention of living well and follows his calling as best he can may have it said of him that he evangelizes, that is he announces good things. It seems to me that he who lives well proclaims it better than he who speaks well. The former will receive the reward for a good work or a good savour, but the latter, since he knows the will of the Lord and does things worthy of blows,

6 beaten with many stripes, will receive damnation.[5] If anyone should be disturbed that many canons among those who, I say, live next to men do not work with their hands, we can first reply briefly with what the apostle said: 'For bodily exercise is profitable to little, but godliness is profitable to all things.'[6] For when he says bodily exercise profits little, he shows that it is worth something, but not so much that he would impose more than this precept on anyone or would judge anyone who does not work physically to be inferior. But the godliness, which he proclaims as profitable to all things, and which is shown forth among the canons who live among men, is shown forth more greatly by the masters when they are kept in the cloisters; or else, when they go out, they may see the things of this world set beside them, having seen them become attached to them, their weak minds grow soft, and they are destroyed by such a sight. For it is customary to praise cloistered men if they remain long in the cloister and despise

---

[1] 2 Thess. 3: 8. [2] Rom. 1: 9–10. [3] 1 Cor. 9: 14.
[4] 1 Cor. 9: 11. [5] Luke 12: 47. [6] 1 Tim. 4: 8.

et hi qui in claustro sedent aliquid manibus operari uolunt, bonum
hoc esse pronuntio, et otiositatem ab eis sicut a caeteris amputan-
dam esse, iudico, dicens cum apostolo, 'qui non uult operari, nec
manducet.'[1] Hoc enim ita intelligo, quod hoc non solum de
laboribus manuum dicatur, sed etiam de omni opere quod
aecclesiasticis uiris congruit. Quod qui non fecerit, non manducet.
Beata ergo iudicanda est illa uita, quae in claustro sedens, et a
mundanis semetipsam quodammodo incarcerat, et in caelestibus
se ipsam dilatat. Nec ille qui laborat manibus iactet se super eum
qui sedendo laborat, quia in utroque laborem inesse, desidiosi
indicti sunt, qui laborando manibus deficiunt, et sedendo in
claustro torpescunt, testis est etiam nostra infirmitas, quae
laborando lassatur, et contemplando diuina quam citius ad humana
redigitur. Si uero his talibus qui in claustro resident, et prope
homines sunt aliquid operari placuerit, non longius huiusmodi
fratribus est, procedendum, sed circa habitationes suas operandum.
Haec de canonicis qui iuxta homines habitant, pro posse dicta
sufficiant.

VII. *De canonicis qui inter homines seculares habitant et seculares
dicuntur.*

57 De canonicis qui remotius uiuunt, siue de illis qui iuxta homines
morantur superius reddita ratio, ad loquendum de his qui inter
homines habitant nos inuitat, quorum professionem et actus
describere, et uolumus et formidamus. Si enim eos laudare
uoluerimus, sanctioris propositi uiros timemus offendere, qui eos
multociens reprehendunt, si uero uituperare, uerendum est, ne
fratres nostros in eadem fide et christiana deuotione uiuentes,
populumque Dei regentes contristemus. Nolumus autem, nec
nobis conceditur 'ante tempus' quicquam 'iudicare'.[2] Vidimus
enim, et adhuc uidemus multos tales canonicos qui inter homines
uiuunt, propter quod et seculares uocantur, suscepta bona ab
aecclesia fideliter pertractasse, et simplici uictu et uestitu con-
tentos, reliqua pauperibus erogasse, multaque bona uel aecclesiis
uel indigentibus fecisse. Quapropter relinquentes quaedam quae

the sight of worldly things. If they who remain in the cloister also wish to do some work with their hands, I declare this to be good, and I consider that idleness should be denied to them as it is to others, saying with the apostle: 'If any man will not work, neither let him eat.'[1] I understand that this was said not only of manual labour but of all work suitable for men of the church, that he who does nothing shall not eat. That life is to be judged blessed, which keeps within the cloister, sequesters itself to a certain degree from worldly affairs, and extends itself into heavenly ones. And let not him who works with his hands vaunt himself above the man who works seated, since there is labour in both; they have been arraigned for their sloth who are delinquent in manual work and grow sluggish sitting in the cloister: the witness is our weakness, which growing weary in labour and in contemplation of the divine, is all the more quickly brought back to the human. But if it pleases such of these as stay in the cloister, and are near to men, to do any work, they should not go far away from their brothers for this purpose, but should work near their living-places. What I have said as best I can will suffice for the canons who live near men.

VII. *Canons who live among men of the world and are called seculars.*

57 An account has been given above of canons who live away from other men and of those who live near other men, and we must now speak of those who live among men and must describe, though fearfully, their calling and behaviour. If we wished to praise them we should be afraid of offending men of a holier intention, who often speak ill of them. If we wished to insult them, however, we should fear lest we sadden our brothers who live in the same faith and Christian devotion, directing God's people. We do not wish 'to judge anything before the time',[2] nor is it permitted to us. For we have seen and still do see that many such canons, who live among men and are thus called seculars, have managed church property responsibly and, content with simple diets and clothing, have spent the rest on the poor and have done many good things both for the churches and for the needy. On this account, leaving aside some of the things they

---

[1] 2 Thess. 3: 10.   [2] 1 Cor. 4: 5.

faciunt, et minus Deo placere uidentur, ut sunt uestes preciosae
quibus plerique eorum utuntur, et domus superfluo ornatu de-
pictae, necnon negotia quae plerique eorum plus iusto seculariter
exercent, ostendere temptemus Deo auxiliante, quid professio
eorum contineat, quod in aecclesia habeant officium, unde Deo
placeant, quem locum in eius tabernaculo teneant, si tamen quod
suum est impleant. Non enim hoc opere statui aliorum facta
mordaci stilo carpere, sed uniuscuiusque professio quid boni
habeat, et quid simile cum antiquis sanctis uel cum ipso Domino
58 demonstrare. Ac primum ipsum nomen quo seculares uocantur,
quod multis uidetur non in prosperum eis cedere, si possumus
uertamus eis in bonum. Intueamur ergo apostolum Paulum in
epistola ad Hebreos ubi de priori testamento loquitur, quod
'habuit' inquit[a] 'iustificationes culture, et sanctum seculare'.[1]
Vt enim in quodam libro inueni, sanctum seculare locum uocat
atriorum, ubi gentiles ad Iudaismum transeuntes[b] stabant ad
adorandum post Iudeos, quem sine dubio sacerdotes et leuitae
custodiebant. Inspice ergo et istos quos uocamus seculares
canonicos, si non atria aecclesiae forensia custodiunt, si non im-
puros quosque et uero Iudaismo, hoc est uerae fidei confessioni
repugnantes a sanctificatis locis arceant, et excommunicando pro
auctoritate sibi tradita expellant. Quibus diligenter perspectis,
intelligere poteris non ex hoc eis competere seculare nomen quod
plerique ex his seculariter uiuant, sed congruenter ideo uocari
seculares, quod seculi homines inter quos uiuunt, regere et in-
formare debeant. Bene igitur facient si de communi uiuant, si superflua a se resecent, et ita canonici id est regulares recte uocabuntur,
optime etiam facient, si commissas sibi oues id est seculares
homines fideliter gubernare studuerint, ita enim nomen seculare
59 eis parum oberit. Dico etiam in nullo debere discrepare eos ab his
qui iuxta homines morantur, nisi forte quis dicat eos plus debere
laxari,[c] et plurima loca frequentare, ut pluribus prodesse possint,
qui super plures primatum accipiunt. Caeterum in aliis rebus id

---

[a] inquit *add. supra*   [b] transeuntes ad Iudaismum *corr.* ad Iudaismum
transeuntes   [c] laxari *add. supra*

do which seem to please God less, as for example the costly clothing which many of them wear, and houses painted with an excess of ornament, and the secular activities in which many of them indulge more than seems fitting, we shall try to show, with God's help, what their calling consists in, what their duties in the church are, whereby they please God, what place they hold in His tabernacle, provided that they carry out God's will. I have not intended in this work to carp at the deeds of others with a biting pen but to demonstrate what is good in each calling and what 8 is similar in them to the ancient saints or to the Lord. But first we shall, if we can, make good use of the name by which the seculars are known, which for many does not seem to say anything favourable about them. Let us see what the apostle Paul in his letter to the Hebrews says when he speaks of the Old Testament, that it 'indeed had also justifications of divine service and a worldly sanctuary'.[1] For, as I have found in a certain book, the worldly sanctuary is called the place of the courtyards, where the gentiles converted to Judaism stood to worship after the Jews, and of which the priests and levites doubtless were in charge. See therefore if those whom we call secular canons are not also in charge of the outer courtyards of the church, if they do not keep those who are impure and repugnant to true Judaism, that is to the true faith, at a distance from the sanctified places and expel them by excommunication with the authority granted to them. Having examined these matters carefully, you will understand that the name secular does not stem from the fact that many of them live secular lives, but they are called seculars suitably because they must direct and instruct the men of the world among whom they live. They will do well, then, if they live communally, if they cut off superfluous things from their lives, and then they will properly be called canons, that is regulars. And they will do best if they strive faithfully to govern the sheep entrusted to them, that is 9 the men of this world. In this case the name secular will damage them but little. I say that one should make no distinction between them and those who live next to men, unless perhaps someone should say that they ought to live less restricted lives and frequent more places in order to be of use to more people by taking charge of more people. For the rest, I consider that they ought to be

[1] 9: 1. The N.E.B. version reads: 'The first Covenant indeed had its ordinances of divine service and its sanctuary, but a material sanctuary.'

est in uestitu et habitu et moribus decerno consimiles esse debere.
Sed tamen ita temperate de eis loqui debemus, ut quod in eis
corrigendum est et continuo corrigi non potest, quia ita inoleuit
consuetudo toleretur, quod uero in eis bonum est et acceptum Deo
laudetur. Relicta igitur mordaci reprehensione quae auditoribus
forsitan scandalum generaret, et illis canonicis nichil forte pro-
desset, consideremus eorum in aecclesia officium, intueamur et
locum, et ex libro numeri ut proposuimus similitudinem horum
trahamus. Et quia filios Caath qui remotius et secretius Deo in
tabernaculo eius seruiebant, remotioribus canonicis assimilauimus,
et Gersonitas qui aliquid interius et aliquid exterius in officio
habebant canonicis qui iuxta homines sunt[a] et plus interius et
minus exterius habent comparauimus, nunc de filiis Merari qui
et ipsi interius et exterius in tabernaculo Dei ministrabant, ad
canonicos quos secundum rationem superius dictam seculares
60 appellari uolumus, similitudinem trahamus. Primum autem
uideamus, quid Merari nomen indicet, ut postea quomodo canonicis talibus conueniat agnoscamus. Merari enim interpretatur
amaricans, siue amaritudo.[1] Et isti canonici similiter qui populos
regunt, qui immundos de aecclesia expellunt, qui redeuntibus ad
aecclesiam paenitentiam indicunt, qui omnia transitoria despicienda
predicant, qui iniquis paenas inferni nisi resipuerint proponunt,
quid aliud quam amaricantes dici possunt? Amaricant enim se
ipsos, cum mala et peccata sua uel populorum in se commissa
uel aliis illata deplorant, amaricant et sibi commissos, cum eos
pro culpis de coetu fidelium expellunt, uel cum satisfacientes
paenitentiae laboribus onerant. Et quia ex oneribus eorum officia
cognoscimus, uideamus a quo tempore onera ferre incipiant, ut
postea quae sint eorum onera perpendamus. Nam et ipsi 'a
triginta annis[b] et supra usque ad annum quinquagesimum'[2]
ministrare sicut caeteri precipiuntur, ut in eis et perfectio uirtutis
61 et mortificatio carnis inesse debere monstretur. Portant autem
'tabulas tabernaculi et uectes, columnas et bases earum, columpnas quoque atrii cum basibus et paxillis et funibus suis. Omnia
uasa et suppellectilem ad numerum accipiunt' precipiente Domino,

---

[a] qui . . . sunt *add. in marg.*   [b] annis *add. supra*

similar in other matters, that is in clothing, way of living, and customs. However, we must speak of them with such moderation that what there is in them to be corrected which cannot be corrected immediately, since it is sanctified by custom, should be tolerated, and what is good in them and acceptable to God should be praised. Avoiding sharp criticism, then, which could give rise to scandal among our listeners and which would in no way help the canons, let us consider their duties in the church. Let us consider the place and, as we have proposed, make a comparison with them from the book of Numbers. And since we have compared the sons of Caath who served God in his tabernacle in solitude and at a distance from men to the more distant canons, and the Gersonites, who carry out some internal and some external duties, to the canons who live next to men and have more internal and fewer external tasks, let us now compare the sons of Merari, who served both inside and outside God's tabernacle, to the canons whom, following the account given above, we wish to call seculars.

60 First let us see what the name Merari signifies and then let us discover how it fits such canons. Merari means making bitter or bitterness,[1] and these canons, like those who govern the people, who expel the impure from the church, who impose penance on those men returning to the church, who preach contempt for all things transitory, who explain the punishments of hell to the unrepentant wicked, what else can they be called but makers of bitterness? For they make themselves bitter when they deplore their own evil-doing and sin or those of the people committed on themselves or inflicted on others, and they make bitter those committed to them when they expel them from the community of the faithful for their sins, or burden them with the labours of penitence when they are making satisfaction. And since we know the offices from their burdens, let us see at what time they begin to bear burdens, so that afterwards we may consider what their burdens are, for they too are ordered to minister like the others 'from thirty years old and upward unto fifty years old',[2] so that the perfection of virtue and the mortification of the flesh should be shown displayed

61 in them. They carry 'the boards of the tabernacle and the bars, the pillars and their sockets, the pillars also of the court with their sockets and pins and cords. They shall receive by account all the

[1] Jerome, *Nom. heb.* (*CC.* lxxii. 76).
[2] Num. 4: 30.

'et sic portant.'[1] Si consideremus diligenter Meraritarum onera,
inueniemus ea fuisse grauia, quamobrem et illos in ueteri lege
fortes in preceptis Domini custodiendis fuisse oportet, quibus
tam grauia et tam digna onera commissa sunt. Si autem illi in
preceptis Domini fortes dicendi sunt, qui in umbra futuri Deo
seruiebant, quantomagis illi qui in ueritate aecclesiam eius
supportare in officio susceperunt? Et si quem mouet, quod filios
Merari canonicis qui inter homines uiuunt assimilamus, et illorum
onera officiis istorum comparamus, intendat diligenter si aliquid
congruum haec dicentes inuenimus. Et quia superius diximus
Meraritas interius et exterius ministrasse, uide si non etiam
canonici qui inter homines sunt hoc faciunt. Ministrant enim
interius, cum in aecclesia officia aecclesiastica gradatim accipiunt,
ut in domo Dei cotidie illi seruiant, ministrant et exterius, cum
plebes Dei ad aecclesiam aduocant, instruunt precepta iniungunt,
quid unoquoque die in aecclesia facere, quid in domo, quid in
agro, debeant, utrum uacare an operari, ieiunare an manducare
possint indicant. Preterea contemptores dominicorum preceptorum
suorumue de aecclesia expellunt, correctos reuocant, incorrectos
condempnant, ut ne ad mortem quidem communionem accipiant,
nec sepulturam in sacratis locis habeant. Talia autem officia quae
enumerauimus, intus et foris ut perspicuum est canonici qui
dicuntur seculares exercent. Vnde merito tales si officium suum
bene impleuerint, portitoribus tabularum tabernaculi et uectium,
columpnarum et basium, columpnarum quoque atrii, basiumque
et paxillorum et funium adaequari possunt. Tabulatum etenim
tabernaculi portant, cum sanctorum patrum opera et scripta
quibus aecclesiam Dei portauerunt et decorauerunt, populis
sibi commissis ad exemplum proponunt, et docent quia sicut
tabernaculum super tabulas innitebatur affixum, sic aecclesia stat
innixa uerbis et operibus apostolorum et prophetarum. Portant
et uectes quibus tabulae firmabantur, ut structura superimposita
non moueretur, cum testimonia et precepta quae data sunt nobis
custodienda ut in eis firmiter hereamus populis proponunt.
Ferunt et columpnas, cum doctores qui prophetas et apostolos

vessels and furniture' on God's command 'and carry them.'[1]
If we carefully consider the burdens of the Merarites we shall
find that they were heavy ones. And for this reason it was fitting
that those to whom such heavy and worthy burdens were committed under the old law should be strong in keeping the Lord's
commands. If those who served God in the shadow of the future
should be called strong in God's commands, how much more
should those who in the time of truth took up the duty of main-
taining His church? And if it should disturb anyone that we have
compared the sons of Merari to the canons who live among men,
and the burdens of office of the one to those of the other, let him
see carefully whether we have found anything fitting by saying
these things—and since we have said above that the Merarites
served inside and outside, see whether the canons also do not do
this. For they minister inside when they take up ecclesiastical
duties in the church one after the other, so as to serve every day
in God's house, and they minister outside when they call God's
people to church, instruct them, lay down what they must do
every day in church, at home, and in the fields, whether they may
take their ease or work, fast or eat. Further, they expel from the
church those who despise the Lord's commands or theirs; they
recall the corrected and condemn the recalcitrant, lest they receive
communion at death or have burial in consecrated ground. Such
duties as we have enumerated, interior and exterior, are carried
out, as is evident, by secular canons. For this reason such men,
if they have fulfilled their office properly, can be compared to the
carriers of the boards of the tabernacle, and the bars, the pillars,
and the sockets, the pillars also of the courtyard, and sockets and
pins and cords. Indeed they carry the boards of the tabernacle
when they teach and explain as examples to the people committed
to them the works and writings of the Fathers, by which they have
carried and decorated the church of God, since just as the tabernacle was supported by being fixed to boards, the church stands
supported by the words and works of the apostles and prophets.
They carry also the bars by which the boards are made firm so
that the structure on the top was not moved, when they explain
to the people the testimonies and precepts, which have been given
to us to keep so that we shall stand firmly in them. They bear
the pillars when they teach the people to imitate the doctors who

[1] Num. 4: 31–2.

sequuti sunt, qui etiam ipsi aecclesiam Dei portauerunt, populis imitandos esse edocent. Bases quoque columpnarum deferunt, cum regimen quod aecclesia semper habuit, plebibus ostendunt. Basis enim dicitur rex. Et attende diligenter, quid postea de Meraritis sequatur, quia columpnas atrii per circuitum cum basibus et paxillis et funibus suis portant. Cum enim superius tabulas tabernaculi et uectes et columpnas et bases portare dicebantur, demonstrabatur eos in interioribus tabernaculi aliquid habuisse officii. Cum uero columpnas atrii cum basibus et paxillis et funibus portare memorantur, potestatem super plebes quae ad tabernaculum conueniebant, et extra tabernaculum erant, tenuisse indicantur. Neque enim structuram atriorum ferre,

62   et inordinate in atriis se habentes non cohibere poterant. Vnde quia istos Merari filios canonicis qui seculares dicuntur assimilauimus, uidendum est quia sicut illi in tabernaculo Dei deseruiebant, et rursum extra tabernaculum atria custodiebant, sic et isti interius Deo seruire, et contemplationi studere debent, et exterius propter alios sibi commissos militare, et onera aliorum deferre oportet. Debent etiam sibi subiectis plebibus herere, et sibi commissos non deserere. Hoc enim per paxillos tabernaculo affixos designatur. Funes etiam tabernaculi portare precipiuntur, ut se sibique commissos caritate mutua asstringant. His igitur omnibus perspectis, inspicere potes canonicos quos dicimus seculares, si officium suum quod habent in aecclesia bene custodierint, et professionem suam quam aecclesiae Dei faciunt obseruauerint, non dici debere seculares quod seculariter uiuant, sed quod seculi homines regere debeant. Si enim primum consideremus parentum ipsorum deuotionem, qui filios suos erudiendos in aecclesia offerunt, et si intueamur quales sancta aecclesia post suam doctrinam eosdem postulet ad gradus ordinum promouendos, intelligere poterimus eos non seculariter debere uiuere, qui ideo docentur ut speculatores domus Israel postmodum ponantur.[1] Sed nec illud omittendum est, quod filii Merari sicut in numero legitur, 'omnia uasa et suppellectilem ad numerum accipiebant' cum caeteris oneribus 'sicque portabant'.[2] Hic

followed the prophets and apostles, who have also borne God's church. They also carry the sockets of the pillars when they make known to the people the governance the church has always had. For socket means king. And look at what follows concerning the Merarites carefully, that they carry the pillars of the courtyard round about with their sockets and pins and cords. For when, as was said above, they were to carry the boards of the tabernacle and the bars and the pillars and the sockets, it was shown that they had part of their duty inside the tabernacle. When, however, it was noted that they carried the pillars of the courtyard with their sockets and pins and cords, it was meant that they held power over the people who assembled at the tabernacle and were outside the tabernacle. For they could not carry the building of the courtyards without including those who were disorderly inside the courtyards. And since we have therefore compared those sons of Merari to the canons called seculars, it must be seen that just as the former served zealously in God's tabernacle and in addition looked after the courtyards outside the tabernacle, the seculars in like manner should serve God inside and be zealous in contemplation, and outside fight for those committed to their care and bear the burdens of others. They must also remain close to the people subject to them and never desert those committed to them. This is signified by the pins fixed to the tabernacle. They are also ordered to carry the cords of the tabernacle so that they and those committed to them would be bound to each other in mutual charity. Having looked at all these, you can examine the canons we call seculars to see whether they have discharged their duty in the church well and have observed the calling which they vowed in God's church and are therefore not to be called seculars because they live secular lives but because they must direct secular men. If we first consider the devotion of their parents, who offer their sons to the church to be taught, and if we understand that after teaching them the holy church will ask them to be promoted to the degrees of ordination, we shall be able to comprehend why they who are taught so that they can later be appointed watchmen to the house of Israel should not live secular lives.[1] But one must not forget to say that the sons of Merari, as we read in Numbers, 'received by account all the vessels and furniture' with the other burdens 'and carried them'.[2] Here one can understand what we

---

[1] Ezek. 3: 17; 33: 7.   [2] Num. 4: 32.

intelligi potest etiam illud quod superius de aliis familiis leuitici
ordinis diximus, licet hic non aperte referatur, quod unusquisque
pro uitae merito officium in tabernaculo Dei sortiretur. Neque enim
aestimo sibi conferri debere, eos qui tabulas tabernaculi et bases
et columpnas et uasa ferebant, et eos qui supellectilem in ministerio
suscipiebant. Sed etiam illud uidendum est, quod haec familia
cum dignioribus officiis etiam supellectilem accipiebat, ut
intelligant hi quibus hanc leuitarum familiam comperamus, sui
officii esse, ut nichil quod etiam minimum sit in aecclesia quod ad
se uel ad populos sibi commissos pertineat debere contempni,
sed summo studio agere, ut omnia ordinate et secundum Deum
fiant. Quo enim super plures potestatem accipiunt, eo magis plura
et maiora et minora curare debent, reminiscentes quia 'cui
63 multum commissum est, multum requiretur ab eo'.¹ Sed ne illos
quidem sacerdotes relinquere debemus, qui a pontificibus ordinati,
tanquam ab Aaron et filiis eius ad parroechias gubernandas ab
episcopis uel eorum ministris mittuntur, et illis obaedientes existunt.
Non enim debet eorum uita a canonicorum id est regularium
conuersatione discrepare, sed ordinate et regulariter ut rectores
populorum decet inter seculares homines uiuere. Conuenit etiam
his, ut ubicunque inter homines habitant, et ipsi et familiae
eorum se religiosius habeant quam caeteri plebeii homines, ut in
omnibus actibus suis officium suum et ordinem honorent, et
elemosinas fidelium non frustra comedant, sed in omnibus Deum
64 laudabilem faciant. Si autem requiratur a me et horum in antiquis
similitudo, habes superius eos per illos leuitas qui columpnas
et bases atrii ferebant significatos. Nam et atrium in quo mundi
homines adorandum conueniebant iuxta tabernaculum, potest
uniuersalis aecclesiae latitudinem significare, quae ubique per
mundum diffusa tanquam atrium amplum se ipsam prebet, et
portitores suos id est rectores quasi columpnas et bases ferentes
habet. Habes etiam illud exemplum superius memoratum, ubi
dictum est, quod cum sex ciuitatibus fugitiuorum, quadraginta
.VIII. oppida leuitis sunt distributa, quod posse significare eos
qui ad regendos populos et tuendos ab impiis, longe a principibus
sacerdotum mittuntur, superius demonstrauimus. Quod etiam

said earlier about the other families of the levite order, though it is not mentioned explicitly, that everyone was allotted a duty in God's tabernacle in accordance with the merits of his life. For I do not believe that they who carried the boards of the tabernacle and the sockets and the pillars and the vessels, and they who took up the furniture in their ministry, would have conferred this duty on themselves. But one must see that this family also accepted the furniture along with the more worthy offices, so that they to whom we have compared this levite family should understand that it is their duty to see that nothing in the church, however small, which pertains to them or to the people committed to them, is despised but is done with the greatest zeal, so that everything is carried out in an orderly way and according to God. For as they receive power over many, the more they should care for many things both great and small, remembering that 'to whom they have committed much, of him will they demand 63 the more'.[1] But we must not leave aside those priests who, ordained by the pontiffs, as by Aaron and his sons, are sent by bishops or their ministers to direct parishes and who live in obedience to them. For their life ought not to differ from the way of life of the canons, that is the regulars, but they should live among secular men as mentors of the people in an orderly and regular fashion. It is suitable for them that wherever they live among men, both they and their households should conduct themselves more religiously than the rest of the common people, so that in all their actions they do honour to their office and their order and do not consume the alms of the faithful in vain but make God praise-64 worthy in all they do. If a likeness from antiquity is required from me for them too, you have one above signified by those levites who carried the pillars and sockets of the courtyard. For the courtyard where clean men gathered to pray next to the tabernacle can represent the breadth of the universal church, which shows itself spread over the whole world like a vast courtyard and of which the carriers, that is the mentors, are like the pillars and sockets. You have the example noted above, where it is said that the forty-eight towns of the levites were distributed with the six cities for fugitives, which we have shown above can signify those who are sent afar by the principal priests to rule the people and protect them from the ungodly. This can also now suitably be

[1] Luke 12:48; cf. Benedict, *Reg.*, II, 30.

nunc de his, congrue potest intelligi. A matrice enim aecclesia
quasi a tabernaculo, et a pontificibus quasi a filiis Aaron accipiunt
65 potestatem regendi populos. Si autem requiras a me de illis qui
solummodo clerici uocantur et canonici non sunt quomodo uiuere
debeant, legere potes Ieronimi librum ad Nepotianum, et alium
equidem ad Oceanum, lege etiam Ysidori libellum de aecclesiasticis
officiis, et uidere poteris qualiter se agere debeant. Sed ut ad^a
canonicos de quibus nobis sermo est redeamus, ne illud quidem
omittendum est, quod 'duo' tantum 'plaustra et quatuor boues
filiis Gerson' ad deferenda onera dati sunt, his autem id est 'filiis
Merari, quatuor plaustra et .VIII. boues' tributa sunt.¹ Forsitan
enim per hoc ostenditur, quia sicut Gersonitae minus terrena
curabant et minus a terrenis hominibus recipiebant, sic canonici
qui iuxta homines sunt, quos per Gersonitas significari posse
diximus, quia minus terrena curant, minus a terrenis recipiunt.
Filii autem Merari qui illos canonicos significant qui de secularibus
hominibus magis solliciti sunt, plura adiumenta a secularibus
accipiunt, et per hoc illos indicant, qui secularium multiplicius
66 curam gerentes, maiora bona temporalia ab eis accipiunt. Si
autem tacitus quis apud semetipsum dicat, quare ergo canonici
qui dicuntur seculares in matrice^b aecclesiis positi, potestatem
super alios etiam sanctioris propositi uiros id est super canonicos
et monachos habent, et quasi primi in tabernaculo Dei sunt, cum
etiam religiosioribus precepta iniungunt, sicut faciunt decani et
archidiaconi, de hoc breuiter possum respondere, quia canonicalis
ordo antiquitus aliquantulum tepuerat, et oportebat ut illi qui
de hoc ordine inueniebantur, regendas aecclesias plebesque
susciperent. Nunc autem si etiam aliis canonicis sanctioris
propositi et monachis presunt, non se debent efferre quasi digniores
sint, sed modeste se habere, et illos credere digniores quos Deus
magis postposita seculari sollicitudine sibi paucisque sibi commissis seruire elegit, et temporalia parum curare. Perspice etiam
Meraritas sub manu Ithamar filii Aaron summi sacerdotis qui
interpretatur amaritudo esse constitutos, ut intelligant canonici
qui Meraritis assimilantur potestatem quam super plebes Dei
habent, non sibi debere dulcescere, sed cum necessitas exerendae
potestatis incumbit propter subiectorum obstinationem, tunc

---

^a ad *add. supra*   ^b matricis *corr.* matrice

understood of these men. They accept the power of directing the people from the mother church and from the pontiffs, just as if from the tabernacle and the sons of Aaron. If you ask me how they who are only called clerics and not canons should live, you can read Jerome's book to Nepotianus, and likewise the other to Oceanus. Read also Isidore's book on ecclesiastical offices and you will see how they should behave. But so that we may return to the canons, of whom we are speaking, we must not omit concerning them that only two wagons and four oxen were given to Gerson's sons for carrying burdens. To the others, however, that is to the sons of Merari, four wagons and eight oxen were given.[1] Perhaps this shows that the Gersonites cared less for earthly things and received less from men of the world. Thus the canons who live next to men, and who can be said to be represented by the Gersonites, care less for earthly things and so receive less from men of the world. But the sons of Merari, who represent those canons who care more for secular men, receive more assistance from secular men, and through this they show that those who bear more care for secular men accept more worldly goods from them. If anyone should say quietly to himself, why do the canons who are called seculars and who are in mother churches have power over men of more holy life, that is over canons and monks, and come as it were first in God's tabernacle, also giving commands to more religious men, as do deans and archdeacons, I can reply briefly that of old the order of canons had grown somewhat lukewarm and it was suitable that the men who were found in that order should be put in charge of churches and the common people. However, if they are nowadays set over other canons of holier life and monks, they should not be puffed up, as if they were more worthy, but should conduct themselves modestly and believe those whom, since they have set aside more completely secular cares, God has chosen to serve Himself and the few committed to Him and to pay less heed to earthly things. See also that the Merarites were instituted under the power of Ithamar, Aaron's son, the high priest, which means bitterness, so that the canons who are compared to the Merarites might understand that they should not let the power they have over God's people become pleasurable to them, but that when it becomes necessary for them to exercise power, because of obstinancy on

[1] Num. 7: 7–8.

debere tristari et amaricari, et 'cum timore et tremore'[1] suam
67 ipsorum salutem operari. Ecce de canonicis qui dicuntur seculares
prout potuimus secundum umbram ueritatis id est ueterem legem
loquuti sumus, quid de his etiam secundum ipsam ueritatem
quae Christus est dicemus? Consideremus illum leuitam uel
sacerdotem 'quem pater sanctificauit et misit in mundum',[2] si
aliquid fecit, quod canonicorum talium professioni uel ordini
congruere possit. Pascha celebraturus immo ipse uerum pascha
futurus, quia 'pascha nostrum immolatus est Christus',[3] in
ciuitatem hoc fecit parari dicens discipulis: 'Ecce introeuntibus
uobis in ciuitatem, occurret uobis homo amphoram aquae portans.
Sequimini eum in domum in quam intrat, et dicite patri familias
domus: Dicit tibi magister: Vbi est diuersorium ubi pascha cum
discipulis meis manducem? Et ipse ostendet uobis cenaculum
magnum stratum, et ibi parate. Euntes autem inuenerunt sicut
dixit illis, et parauerunt pascha.'[4] Repetamus ab initio capitulum
hoc quod proposuimus, et conferamus discipulos domini Iesu ex
precepto Domini introeuntes in ciuitatem, canonicis qui inter
homines habitant, ut pascha celebrent, id est transitum de morte
ad uitam[5] faciendum hominibus secularibus proponant. Ipse
enim ingressus eorum in ciuitatem, dominum[a] pacis[6] demonstrat
per ministros aecclesiae suae inter homines querere habitaculum,
quod fit quando canonici uel quilibet serui Dei ab hominibus
suscipiuntur. Homo uero qui discipulis in ciuitatem introeuntibus
cum amphora uel mensura aquae occurrit, potest indicare eos
qui uenientibus in aliquo loco Dei seruis, modum mundationis
et sanctificationis quo indigent ostendunt, seque per gratiam Dei
iam esse habiles ut Christus in hospicium ubi manent dignetur
intrare, et pascha uerum cum seruis suis celebrare. Et notandum
quod ille qui amphoram portabat pater familias non erat, sed
quasi unus e familia qui iam aquam ministeriis paschalibus
deferret. Vnde credo illum patrem familias hospitalem fuisse

---

[a] uel filium *add. supra* dominum

the part of their charges, then they should become sad and bitter and should work for their salvation 'with fear and trembling'.[1] And so we have spoken of the canons called seculars as best we could, according to the shadow of truth, that is the old law. What then can also be said of them according to the truth itself, that is Christ? Let us consider the levite or priest 'whom the Father hath sanctified and sent into the world'[2] to see whether He did anything which seems suitable to the calling and order of such canons. When He was about to celebrate the Passover, He who Himself was to be the true Passover, 'for Christ our Pasch is sacrificed',[3] He had it prepared in the city, saying to His disciples: 'Behold as you go into the city, there shall you meet a man carrying a pitcher of water: follow him into the house where he entereth in. And you shall say to the goodman of the house: The master saith to thee: Where is the guestchamber, where I may eat the Pasch with my disciples? And he will show you a large dining room, furnished. And there prepare. And they going, found as he said to them and made ready the Pasch.'[4] Let us go over from the beginning the chapter which we have set forth, and let us compare the disciples of the Lord Jesus entering the city at the Lord's command to the canons who live among men, so that they may celebrate the Pasch, that is that they may represent to secular men the transition from death to life.[5] For their entry into the city shows the Son of peace[6] seeking a home among men through the servants of His church, and this is done whenever the canons or any other servants of God are given hospitality by men. But the man carrying the pitcher or measure of water, who met the disciples as they went into the city, can signify those who show to the servants of God when they come into any place the means of cleansing and sanctifying which they lack, and show themselves to be already suitable, by the grace of God, for Christ to deign to enter the inn where they are staying and to celebrate the true Pasch with His servants. And one should note that the man who carried the pitcher was not the goodman but was like one of his household who was already bringing water for the paschal services. For this reason I believe that this goodman, whoever he may have been, was hospitable and sent such a servant for water who would

---

[1] Ephes. 6: 5.   [2] John 10: 36.   [3] 1 Cor. 5: 7.
[4] Luke 22: 10–13.   [5] Jerome, *In Matt.* (*PL*, xxvi. 190c).
[6] Luke 10: 6.

quicunque ille fuerit, et seruum talem ad aquam misisse, qui
aduentantes benigne susciperet, et in domum domini sui fidenter
deduceret. Deduxit autem eos in domum, non solum in domum
eos inducens, sed etiam quia hospitales esse debeant[a] indicans.
Ideo enim dominus Iesus discipulis precipit, ut eum in domum
in quam intrat sequantur, id est, ut hominem secularem et iam
hospitalitati deditum, ipsi qui religiosi uidentur imitari debeant.
Si enim aliquod bonum opus seculares habent in quo precellant,
in hoc etiam sanctis uiris imitabiles sunt. Nam sunt multi tales
in seculo sancti uiri, qui Deum in cordibus habent, et opera Dei
faciunt, sicut fuit Cornelius centurio, qui antequam baptizaretur
erat 'faciens elemosinas multas plebi, et deprecans Deum semper'.[1]
Vnde contigit, ut post uisionem angelicam Petrum discipulorum
Domini principem hospitio susciperet, et baptismum ab eo
perciperet.[2] Sic et multi alii in seculo serui Dei bona opera faciunt,
sed uenientibus ad se religiosis uiris, in bono opere perficiuntur,
sicque saluantur. Sepe etiam contingit seruis Dei, ut uenientes
ad aliquem locum Dei seruitio aptum, statim inueniant aliquos
ibi qui eos suscipiant, a quibus etiam locum ad habitandum
accipiant, ut ibi Iesus cum discipulis pascha manducet, et sacra-
mentum corporis et sanguinis sui quomodo celebrari debeat
instituat. Vnde et subditur: 'Et ipse ostendet uobis cenaculum
68 magnum stratum, et ibi parate.'[3] Hic inspicere licet, quod cenaculum magnum stratum mentem eorum qui Christum pauperem
cum seruis suis suscipiunt, et in suis habitationibus ad aedificanda
monasteria locum prebent, mentem iam a terrenis eleuatam
habent, unde dicitur quia ipse homo cenaculum ostendit quod in
superioribus semper constat. Magnum uero est, quia dilatato suo
animo illud[b] offerunt. Stratum uero, quia ad omnia pro nomine
69 Domini predicando et dilatando paratum est. Sequitur uero in
euangelio: 'Euntes autem discipuli, inuenerunt sicut dixit illis, et
parauerunt pascha.'[4] Cum enim serui Dei ueniunt ad ciuitates uel
loca ubi christiani morantur, si ueraciter Dei serui sunt, inueniunt
fideles qui eos suscipiant, qui eis ad seruiendum Deo loca pre-
beant, ut ibi pascha preparent, id est homines inter quos uiuunt,

---

[a] debeant *add. supra*   [b] illud *add. supra*

kindly receive those who came in and lead them faithfully into the house of his master. He led them into the house then, not only bringing them into the house but also indicating to them that they should be guests there. For the Lord Jesus therefore commanded His disciples that they should follow him into the house he would enter, that is that those who seem religious should imitate a man of the world already devoted to hospitality. For if men of the world have any good work in which they excel they can be imitated in it by holy men. For there are many such holy men in the world, who have God in their hearts and do God's work, as did Cornelius the centurion, who before he was baptized was 'giving much alms to the people and always praying to God'.[1] And so it happened that after the angelic vision, he received Peter, the prince of the disciples of the Lord, in his house and received baptism from him.[2] And there are many other servants of God in the world who do good works, but after religious men have come to them they are perfected in good works and are thus saved. It often happens to servants of God that, coming to some place suitable for God's service, they immediately find people there who take them in, from whom they also receive a place to live, so that Jesus might eat the Pasch with His disciples there and institute the proper celebration of the sacrament of His body and blood. This is why the words are added: 'And he will show you a large dining-room, furnished. And there prepare.'[3] Here one may see that the large dining-room, furnished, [signifies] the mind of those who receive the poor Christ with His servants and offer them a place in their lands for the building of monasteries, and already have a mind elevated above earthly things, wherefore it is said that this man shows them a dining-room, which is always on the upper storey. It is large indeed, because they offer it with an enlarged soul. It is furnished, because it was prepared for all things in God's name by being preached and spread abroad. There follows in the Gospel: 'And they going found as he had said to them and made ready the Pasch.'[4] For when God's servants come to cities or places where Christians live, if they are really God's servants, they find members of the faithful who receive them, who allot to them places for God's service, so that they will prepare the Pasch there, that is men among whom they live and whom

---

[1] Acts 10: 1–2.   [2] Acts 10: 48.
[3] Luke 22: 12.   [4] Luke 22: 13.

'de morte ad uitam' transire[1] doceant. Tale pascha desiderat Iesus cum discipulis manducare, 'ut faciat' in hominibus 'uoluntatem 70 eius qui misit illum', et 'ut perficiat opus eius'.[2] Sed dicit michi aliquis: Quam conuenientiam ostendis de hoc capitulo euangelico ad canonicos qui inter homines uiuunt? Numquid ista omnia non possunt habere alias significationes, et aliis seruis Dei congruere? Respondeo ad ista: Scio quidem haec ab expositoribus sanctis aliter pertractata, sed in his est quiddam canonicis istis congruum, quia et Iesus cum discipulis introiuit in ciuitatem, et mansit in domo quadam ciuitatis, et hoc in cenaculo illius domus, et ibi cum discipulis pascha celebrauit, et sacramenta corporis et sanguinis sui tradidit. Perpende igitur canonicos qui inter homines uiuunt si non similiter faciunt uel facere debent. Introeunt enim in ciuitatem ut pascha celebrent, id est uiam 'de morte ad uitam'[1] sequendam ostendant, manent in domo cuiusdam, cum unius pre caeteris deuotio eis domum ad habitandum facit, et[a] in possessione sua et aecclesiam et domum faciendam concedit. Ostendit et cenaculum magnum stratum, cum talem locum aptum supernis officiis demonstrat. Potest etiam iste quidam homo euangelicus plures indicare, uel plures esse, sed unus dicti sunt, propter unanimem erga Deum et seruos eius uoluntatem. In tali etiam loco pascha a discipulis preperatur, et ab Iesu desiderabiliter manducatur, cum mansiones fratribus Deo seruientibus aptantur, ut in conuentu fratribus psallentibus et orantibus, et in nomine domini Iesu congregatis, in medio eorum 71 deambulans, ipsorum profectibus reficiatur. De domibus etiam communibus quas plures eorum non habent, si a me requiras, quid respondeam nescio, nisi forte quis uelit dicere, eos et singulatim posse manere, et de communi posse uiuere. Hoc enim et apud antiquos heremitas inuenimus, quorum plerique per cellulas suas manebant, et tamen de communi uiuebant. Si autem hic similiter fieret, nichil aut parum cellulae uel domus diuisae obessent. Sed cum unusquisque familiam suam aggregat, insuper et mulieres secum manere permittunt, tu ipse uides quid inde contingat. Sed ut aliquid etiam congruum de habitationibus eorum dicamus, quorum bona laudare uolumus et diligere, in pluribus

---

[a] uel *add. supra* et (vel *Martène*)

they teach to pass over 'from death to life'.[1] Jesus desires to eat
such a Pasch with His disciples, so that among men He may 'do
70 the will of him that sent him and perfect his work'.[2] But someone
says to me: What have you shown of this chapter of the gospel
which is applicable to the canons who live among men? Surely
all this can have other meanings and be applied to other servants
of God? I reply to that: I know that this has been interpreted
differently by other holy expositors of scripture, but there is in
these things something suitable for the canons, since both Jesus
and His disciples entered the city and stayed in a certain house of
the city and in a dining-room of this house and celebrated the
Passover with His disciples and delivered to them the sacraments
of His body and blood. Think of the canons who live among
men and see whether they do not do, or should not do, the same.
For they enter cities to celebrate the Pasch, that is they show the
way to be followed 'from death to life';[1] they stay in somebody's
house, whenever the devotion of one more than others gives them
a house to live in or lets them build a church or house on his
property. He shows them a large dining-room, furnished, when
he shows such a place fitted for heavenly offices. This certain
evangelical man can indicate many, or be many, but these are to
be one, because of their single will towards God and His servants.
In such a place, also, the Pasch is prepared by the disciples and is
eaten by Jesus with desire, when the lodgings are adapted to the
brothers serving God, so that in the monastery with the brothers
praying and singing psalms and gathered in the name of the Lord
Jesus, he walking in their midst may be refreshed by their progress.
71 Concerning the communal buildings, which many of them do not
have, if you ask me anything about them, I do not know how to
answer, unless perhaps someone would like to say that they can
both lodge singly and live from the common property. For we also
find this among the hermits of old, of whom many lodged in their
cells and nevertheless lived from the common property. If it should
be done here likewise, cells or divided houses would present no
obstacle, or only a small one. But when each gathers his household,
and moreover women are allowed to live with them, you yourself
can see what will come of it. But so that we can say something
fitting about the lodgings of those men, whose good aspects we
desire to praise and love, the location of their lodgings is in many

[1] 1 John 3: 14.   [2] John 4: 34.

locis ipse locus habitationis eorum aecclesiarum fabricae est
contiguus, et claustrum appellatur. Audiuimus etiam in pluribus
locis obseruari, ne quid in toto illo spacio seculare agatur, ne
quid a quoquam iocosum aut minus religiosum fiat, feminas etiam
ab illis locis arceri. Et gratias Deo, quod etiam in hoc ordine
plures inueniuntur, qui ordinem suum aliquantisper honorant.
Habent etiam plures eorum aliquantas communes domos, ut est
claustrum et refectorium, et frequenter et ᵃ sepius simul comedunt.
Audiui etiam quosdam simul quiescere. Qui autem bene faciunt,
alios sui ordinis uiros ad similia inuitent, qui autem adhuc infirmi
72 sunt, fortiores imitentur. Si autem requiratur quem tales canonici
post Christum et eius apostolos patrem institutionis huius et
ordinis sui debeant appellare, nullum alium melius inuenimus
licet multi precesserint qui clericorum patres fuerint, quam beatum
Augustinum. Ex eo enim quod prope ciuitatem Ypponiensem
aecclesiam fratrum 'secundum regulam sub sanctis apostolis
constitutam instituit',ᴵ pater illorum qui iuxta homines sunt
recte appellatur, ex eo uero quod in episcopio positus cum
fratribus etiam communiter uixit, eorum etiam qui inter plebes
cum episcopis uel sub episcopis degunt, pater fuisse iure dicetur.
Extant etiam sermones eius de uita clericorum habiti, ubi apparet
et eos qui ante episcopatum eius cum eo uixerunt, et eos qui in
episcopatu cum eo manserunt, simili modo communiter et
regulariter uixisse.² Quod autem in hoc ordine agitur de quo
loquimur si bonum est teneatur, si uero prauum corrigatur, ut
Christus in eis laudetur, ut cum uenerit iudex omnium, 'unusquisque in suo ordine'³ resurgens, premia aeterna consequatur.
Precor autem caritatem tuam quicunque haec legis, si talis es
cui Deus tribuat intellectum, si aliquid boni inueneris benedic
Dominum, si uero aliquid dissonum et incongruum inueneris,
statim corrige quod notabile reppereris.

73   Descriptis igitur duobus tripertitis ordinibus monachorum et
canonicorum quorum particio prima dicitur heremitarum, qui
frequenter et a ueteribus monachi appellati sunt, uno autem qui
non est in numero aecclesiasticae regulae id est monachorum

ᵃ uel *add. supra* et (etiam *Martène*)

places next to the building of a church and is called a cloister. We have heard that in many places care is taken that nothing secular is done in the entire area and nothing frivolous or irreligious is done by anyone; women are kept at a distance from these places. And, thanks to God, many are also found in this order who for a time honour their order. Many of them have some communal buildings, such as a cloister and refectory, and eat together from time to time. I have heard also that some of them sleep together. Those who do well, let them invite other men of their order to do likewise; those who are as yet weak, let them imitate the stronger. If it is asked whom, after Christ and His apostles, such canons should call the father of this institution and its rules, we have found no one better, though many have gone before who were fathers of clerics, than St. Augustine. From the fact that he instituted near the city of Hippo a church of brothers 'according to a rule established at the time of the holy apostles',[1] he is justly called the father of those who are near men; from the fact that when he lived in the bishop's house he lived communally with his brothers, he is properly said to be the father of those who live among the people with a bishop or under a bishop. There are sermons of his on the clerical way of life, where it appears that they who lived with him before he became a bishop, and they who lived with him when he was bishop, lived in a similar manner, communally according to a rule.[2] However, whatever is done in this order, of which we have spoken, if it is good, let it be kept, if bad, let it be corrected, so that Christ shall be praised in them, so that when the judge of all shall come 'every one', rising up 'in his own order',[3] may receive his eternal rewards. Therefore I pray your charity, whoever shall read this, if you are such a man to whom God grants understanding, if you find anything good, bless God, if anything disagreeable and unsuitable, correct immediately whatever you find noteworthy.

73   Having described two of the threefold order of monks and canons, of whom the first subdivision is said to be the hermits, who have frequently and by the ancients been called monks, and having only touched on and left aside the one which is not in the number of the ecclesiastical rule, that is the secular monks, and

---

[1] Possidius, *Vita Augustini*, 5 (*PL*, xxxii. 37).
[2] Augustine, *Serm.* 355, 2 (*PL*, xxxix. 1569–70).
[3] 1 Cor. 15: 23.

secularium solummodo tacto et relicto, et de medio aecclesiae
utinam sublato, aliis uero ordinibus pro posse commendatis et
laudatis, hic primus liber professionum uel diuersorum ordinum
qui sunt in aecclesia finem accipiat.

which should be removed from the middle of the church, and having commended and praised the other orders as best I could, let this first book of the orders and different callings which are in the church come to an end.

INDEX

INDEX OF CITATIONS